PHYSICAL EDUCATION AND RECREATION

for the

VISUALLY HANDICAPPED

Revised Edition

DR. CHARLES E. BUELL
Secretary of the
United States Association
for Blind Athletes
Beach Haven Park, New Jersey
with a chapter
on legislation by
Dr. Julian Stein

The American Alliance for Health, Physical Education, Recreation and Dance

The American Alliance for Health, Physical
Education, Recreation and Dance
1900 Association Drive, Reston, VA 22091
ISBN 0-88314-139-6

Purposes of the American Alliance For Health, Physical Education, Recreation and Dance

The American Alliance is an educational organization, structured for the purposes of supporting, encouraging, and providing assistance to member groups and their personnel throughout the nation as they seek to initiate, develop, and conduct programs in health, leisure, and movement-related activities for the enrichment of human life.

Alliance objectives include:

1. Professional growth and development—to support, encourage, and provide guidance in the development and conduct of programs in health, leisure, and movement-related activities which are based on the needs, interests, and inherent capacities of the individual in today's society.

2. Communication—to facilitate public and professional understanding and appreciation of the importance and value of health, leisure, and movement-related activities as they contribute toward human well-being.

3. Research—to encourage and facilitate research which will enrich the depth and scope of health, leisure, and movement-related activities; and to disseminate the findings to the profession and other interested and concerned publics.

4. Standards and guidelines—to further the continuous development and evaluation of standards within the profession for personnel and programs in health, leisure, and movement-related activities.

5. Public affairs—to coordinate and administer a planned program of professional, public, and governmental relations that will improve education in areas of health, leisure, and movement-related activities.

6. To conduct such other activities as shall be approved by the Board of Governors and the Alliance Assembly, provided that the Alliance shall not engage in any activity which would be inconsistent with the status of an educational and charitable organization as defined in Section 501(c) (3) of the Internal Revenue Code of 1954 or any successor provision thereto, and none of the said purposes shall at any time be deemed or construed to be purposes other than the public benefit purposes and objectives consistent with such educational and charitable status. *Bylaws, Article III*

CONTENTS

PART I
What Physical Educators and Recreation Specialists Should Know about Blindness

PART II
Activities for Visually Handicapped Children

PART III

FOREWORD

Thousands of years ago, Nero said, "Inactivity leads to a short life." Dr. Charles Buell, for over 30 years, has been a leading advocate of mainstreaming physically impaired children into regular public school physical education classes. One of the goals of the United States Association for Blind Athletes is to assist public schools in such a mainstreaming program. Wherever it is possible in games and sports, U.S.A.B.A. encourages participation and competition of blind persons with their sighted peers. This book, carefully written by Dr. Buell, will enable public schools and community recreation departments to achieve success in mainstreaming. The book can be used as a guide by professionals, paraprofessionals, and volunteers to organize meaningful physical activity programs for visually impaired children and adults.

No longer is it either necessary or desirable for visually handicapped persons to be segregated from their sighted peers. As we approach the end of the century, it becomes increasingly evident that tremendous progress has been made in integrating handicapped persons in various walks of life. For example, thousands of blind people are employed in a variety of jobs. It is vital that they acquire and maintain physical fitness to be able to keep pace with their sighted peers. This can be attained only through vigorous physical exercise.

Dr. Buell's imaginative and practical ideas have been a rich source of information and inspiration to all who have been interested in the best possible physical education and recreation programs for blind children. In this book, he provides the "how to do it" information for physical educators, special education teachers, recreators, and parents.

A child cannot succeed until given the opportunity to try. If visually impaired children are given the opportunity to show their capabilities, they easily fit into physical education classes at public schools. A few thousand blind people are competing in sports, many of them with their sighted peers. Thus, such competition is feasible. Unfortunately, the activities of many thousands of others in public schools are being severely restricted. This is due to a widespread misunderstanding of blindness and the underestimation of the capabilities of blind persons.

With sports and other physical activities becoming more and more available, and with more and more visually handicapped persons attending public schools, colleges, and universities, the teacher is faced with a challenge to organize and conduct meaningful physical activity programs for them. If these challenges are met, the result will be fuller lives for visually impaired persons. The reward for such success is even greater than it is for teaching able-bodied persons. This book has been written for the purpose of assisting you, the teacher, to willingly accept this challenge.

Arthur Copeland, *President*
United States Association for Blind Athletes

PREFACE

At the present time, visually handicapped individuals have an increasing association with society and are acquiring constantly growing acceptance as useful members of that society. This is in sharp contrast to their degree of public acceptance not too many years ago. With this change in philosophy, a greater number of individuals with various handicapping conditions are now attending public schools and participating in community activities. Provisions are being made to meet their needs in regular and special classes and programs. As a result, greater numbers of instructors and leaders are coming into contact with impaired, disabled, and handicapped students than ever before. Physical educators and recreation personnel are being called upon increasingly to instruct and work with physically handicapped persons.

Physical education and recreation for visually handicapped persons do not differ greatly from programs offered to the majority of people. Of course, there are some unique problems. The more loss of vision a student has, the more he must depend upon his other senses to gain information. Methods used by visually impaired students are not difficult to understand. The biggest problem faced by many physical educators and recreation specialists lies within themselves, not the students. Many find it difficult to give up false concepts of blindness and adopt approaches which will really help the individual participant. Some teachers and recreation specialists have accepted the challenge. With an open mind they have done some reading or sought information from knowledgeable people and have had firsthand experience with one or more visually impaired students. With a healthy attitude toward, and respect for, the students, these teachers and recreation specialists have provided meaningful experiences that have aided visually impaired boys and girls to become useful adults in the community. Thousands of blind adults are employed in a great variety of jobs; so it can be done. Satisfaction gained from such successes is usually much greater for instructors of handicapped children than for those who teach non-handicapped boys and girls.

The teacher or other person instructing visually handicapped students is faced with a unique challenge. If he is a physical educator or recreation specialist, he has knowledge of the many activities and programs of his profession and is aware of the underlying principles of physical activity; he must acquaint himself with some unique methods or approaches and become aware of problems that lack of vision creates. If his training is in special education, he is aware of the needs of visually handicapped students; he must familiarize himself with the tools of physical activity and recreation. If he is a volunteer, paraprofessional, or parent involved in physical education or recreation for visually handicapped children, he may need resource materials on activities, methods, and approaches. All groups need methods concerning motivation, assessing progress, determining achievement or success, and evaluating attainment of goals.

It is to meet the diverse needs of these individuals that this publication is presented as a reference, a resource, or an immediate aid. Although this publication has been developed with public school and community personnel in mind, the contents also can be used by those in residential facilities or other specific programs for visually handicapped persons.

This book is divided into three parts: (1) What Physical Educators and Recreation Specialists Should Know About Blindness, (2) Activities for Visually Handicapped Children, and (3) Bibliography. Part I of the bibliography contains references on physical education and recreation for visually handicapped children; Part II provides references on blindness and the education of blind students. To help readers find practical information, most of the references are annotated.

The reader's attention is directed to approaches and methods which have been successfully used in programs of vigorous physical education for thousands of visually handicapped students in many public schools. Emphasis throughout is on useful, how-to-do-it information; theories, opinions, and small, one-teacher experiments are seldom mentioned. The aim is to assist the reader to locate quickly information he needs.

The best available information indicates that two out of three visually handicapped students in public schools are not being offered programs of vigorous physical activity. Thus, they are being denied opportunities to develop levels of physical fitness and motor proficiency needed to succeed in many of life's activities. To bring information to teachers in schools scattered throughout the United States, a well-publicized, inexpensive publication is needed. It is hoped that this booklet will meet that need.

Teachers everywhere should learn that loss of vision does not rob one of wisdom, health, stamina, strength, character, or personality. When given the opportunity, blind persons assume responsibilities and perform all duties of first class citizens. Visually handicapped individuals become dependent or second class citizens only when schools and society do not fully meet their obligations.

A survey of available literature leaves many gaps regarding physical activities and recreation for visually handicapped children in public schools and community programs. Many articles deal with visually handicapped persons' needs for physical activity; other articles relate experiences of individual physical educators who have taught this group. Some publications deal with several handicapping conditions and present general program concepts or emphasize a specific program area. There is a considerable amount of unpublished information available from individuals working with visually handicapped individuals and groups. These sources have been tapped and results included so others may benefit from success stories, promising practices, and exciting and productive experiences of others.

Bibliographical and resource materials have been gathered which heretofore remained random in their distribution. Some were confined to journals of certain groups, dedicated to one or several phases of teaching or rehabilitation of visually impaired persons, and were not easily accessible or well-known.

The American Alliance for Health, Physical Education, Recreation and Dance and other organizations constantly receive requests for information on physical education and recreation for visually handicapped persons. In most cases, personal letters have been required to answer these requests because published material has not been available. Stemming then from many requests for materials and resources, recognizing recent developments, and admitting the dearth of material available in an organized and systematic basis, AAHPERD presents this publication.

Part I

WHAT PHYSICAL EDUCATORS AND RECREATION SPECIALISTS SHOULD KNOW ABOUT BLINDNESS

Blind people differ from one another just as much as other human beings. There are problems commonly faced by those who have lost part or all of their vision which are different from those of sighted people. In addition, there are problems faced by the blind which differ from those of the partially sighted. Physical educators and recreation specialists should be aware of the main problems and how they are being solved.

Problems of blindness can be divided into three groups. They are, in descending order of importance: (1) the attitudes of people around impaired, disabled, and handicapped persons, such as parents, teachers, and the public; (2) attitudes of those with handicapping conditions themselves; and (3) the physical loss, complete or partial, of vision. Helen Keller once said, "Not blindness, but the attitude of the seeing to the blind is the hardest burden to bear." It still is, according to most blind people. An individual's self-image is formed from feedback from those close to him. If parents and teachers protect a child from every bump and do not expect him to do things for himself, he is likely to regard himself as dependent upon others. Millions of visually handicapped people have adjusted to their physical loss of vision; it was within their power to do so. Unfortunately, it was not within their power markedly to change prevailing attitudes of the public toward them.

Part II

WHAT PHYSICAL EDUCATORS AND RECREATION SPECIALISTS SHOULD KNOW ABOUT BLINDNESS

Chapter 1

PAUSE BEFORE YOU SAY "THE BLIND CAN'T DO THAT"

Senator Jennings Randolph (Dem., W.Va.) said, "The concept of restoring the handicapped to normal useful lives and gainful employment is well accepted, well established, and of proven practicality for those closely involved with the handicapped." It is not, in this writer's opinion, generally accepted by the public.

The reader, like most people, probably grew up with false notions about blindness. It is hoped that this publication will demonstrate the feasibility and desirability of giving all impaired, disabled, and handicapped persons the assistance they need to live normal, independent lives.

With some obvious exceptions, a blind person can do anything anyone else can. Laws prohibit blind people from driving automobiles but not from working as mechanics in auto repair shops. An employer would not hire a sightless photographer, but could use him in processing film, negatives, and prints in the darkroom. Although vision is necessary to perform certain tasks safely and well, public laws and private employment practices bar visually handicapped persons from thousands of jobs which they can perform safely and proficiently. A large segment of the public denies those with handicapping conditions the right to try.

Today there are thousands of blind people participating in industry. Unfortunately, there are as many more thousands who are unemployed and therefore, cannot fully demonstrate their capabilities. The picture is rather similar in the fields of physical education and athletics. Blind athletes have been permitted to compete on the varsities of some clubs, schools, and universities. Some of these athletes are totally blind, while others are legally blind (with one tenth or less normal vision). There are still many schools where legally blind and sightless persons are not permitted to try out for athletic teams. It is hoped that the following paragraphs of the successes of blind people in many sports will encourage all schools to give their students a fair opportunity to make their varsities and include them in vigorous physical education.

Wrestling has a unique place in sports for the blind. Each year at least 5,000 sighted wrestlers compete against blind opponents. In such bouts blind wrestlers win more often than they lose. Every year 25 blind boys place in the top six spots in various state meets around the country. Upon four occasions schools for the blind have won state team wrestling championships. This has not occurred in any other sport.

Many wrestling teams from schools for the blind have compiled outstanding records against public high schools. Only once has a university level group of blind wrestlers been gathered together to compete against collegiate competition. In 1976 a group of United States blind wrestlers defeated the Toronto University Wrestling Club in Canada. The victory was reported in the Toronto papers the following day.

James Mastro, who has very low vision, placed third in NAAU Greco-Roman wrestling and was named as an alternate on the regular U.S. Olym-

James Mastro places third in 1975 NAAU Greco-Roman Wrestling.

pic Greco-Roman Wrestling Team in 1976. Mike Zorick has placed four times in the top four in his weight in national USWF competition. When Doug Blubaugh wrestles he must remove his glasses which lowers his vision to that of legal blindness. In 1960 he won NCAA, NAAU, and Olympic titles, and was selected as Outstanding Wrestler of the World. A few years ago, Doug Blubaugh was elected to the Wrestling Hall of Fame.

Sightless Tony Maczynski of Delaware placed sixth in a national karate championship, and earned the Black Belt. Legally blind Trischa Zorn of Mission Viejo, California has qualified two consecutive years for the NAAU swimming championships. Only one percent of the competitive swimmers in the U.S. are able to achieve this honor. In swimming the 100 and 200 yd. backstroke events in 59.47 and 2:06.64, Zorn has established herself as one of the top 25 backstrokers in the country, blind or sighted. She was elected to the 1981 All-American High School Female Swimming Team. She is the first legally blind female to earn an athletic scholarship at a university.

Trischa Zorn has established herself as one of the top 25 backstrokers in the country by swimming the 100-yard event in 59.47.

Sightless Sven Nahlin earns a living in Sweden as a scuba diver. He brings valuable timber to the surface from the bottom of the Stockholm harbor. He has taught hundreds of sighted children to scuba dive. In the United States, there is a law prohibiting sightless persons from becoming scuba diving instructors.

About 30 years ago, King Nawahi, a sightless man, swam 26 miles from Catalina Island to the California mainland. In 1981, two blind men, Nigel Verbeck, 40, and Gerald Price, 48, water-skied across the English Channel in 3 hours and 45 minutes. The seas were rough and the fog was dense during the 35-mile trip which enabled them to raise about $30,000 for charities for the blind. In 1973 sightless Dennis Moore paddled a canoe solo across the English Channel. Four years earlier he was a member of a relay team of blind swimmers which swam the Channel. Some years ago, Oral Miller was a member of the Princeton University rowing team. Today he is a lawyer and leader of an organization of the blind.

In the Pan-American Games of 1968, sightless Sonny Yates placed second in sky diving. He received directions from the ground through a radio located in his helmet. Since this type of equipment is available to all sky divers, he did not have an unfair advantage.

Suppose a person is totally blind and totally deaf, what kind of a life could he live? Could such an individual be accepted by his able-bodied peers and lead a full and rewarding life? The reply is definitely affirmative. For example, Ricky Joy of California has successfully met this challenge. He is employed on Hewlett Packard's assembly line, manufacturing electronic items. Joy is an avid short-wave radio fan, talking with people all over the world. How does he do it? It is not too much of a problem to send messages in Morse code. The receiving of messages in Morse code is a problem that he solved by building some apparatus which changes sound to electrical pulses so that he can feel the dots and dashes. He is in good physical condition from swimming, bowling, biking with a sighted friend, and performing other exercises.

Recently a 25-year old sightless Norwegian, Tore Nearland, and his 21-year old sighted partner, Maris Voster, tandem cycled around the world in 79 days to set a record for this sort of thing. In 1981, John Dickey, 72, tandem biked across the United States to attend the 50th reunion of his graduating class at Amherst College.

Some years ago, eight blind climbers, accompanied by four sighted guides, hiked through treacherous country to reach the 19,340 foot peak of Mt. Kilimanjaro in Africa. More recently, five blind climbers, Kirk Adams, Sheila Holsworth, Fred Nocesner, Doug Wakefield, and Justin McDevitt reached the 14,410 foot peak of Mt. Rainier in the state of Washington. It was a dangerous trip made under the direction of experienced guides. The purpose of both climbs was to dispel the mistaken notion that the horizons of the handicapped are limited. Afterward, they accepted an invitation from President Ronald Reagan to meet with him at the White House.

In 1979, totally blind John Stratford turned in one of the outstanding running performances of all time. He ran 420 miles from Wellington to Auckland, New Zealand in an elapsed running time of 61½ hours. Few men, blind or sighted, have achieved as much. His feat was an inspiration to the entire country of New Zealand.

A legally blind man, Bill Daniels, defeated all his sighted opponents in a 40-mile run from Arcata to Willow Creek, California. The run was made in 1977 and ascended to an altitude of 4400 feet. This associate professor at Humboldt State University set a new record for the course of 4 hours and 35 minutes.

The San Francisco Bay Area Transit Company employs sightless Harry Cordellos as an information officer. In his spare time, 44-year old Cordellos has run 68 marathons, some in less than 3 hours. He has logged 25,000 miles, equivalent to running around the world at the equator. He runs with a sighted partner and always finishes in the top one-third or higher of the runners, whether there be hundreds or thousands. When Cordellos competed in the Iron Man Triathlon in 1981, he swam 2.4 miles, tandem biked 112 miles, and ran a marathon, all in 16 hours, 22 minutes, and 26 seconds. He was one of the competitors shown on national television. He has run 50 miles in less than 8 hours.

Harry Cordellos holds a personal marathon record of 2 hours, 57 minutes, and 42 seconds.

Leamon Stansell, legally blind, has won letters in track at Lynwood High School in California. He won his league 2-mile championship, and placed fourth in his division in southern California with a time of 10:09.5. He has run the 10K, 6.2 miles, in 34 minutes and 5 seconds.

Janet Rowley is a member of the women's track team at Boston University. She has high jumped over five feet and thrown the discus 24.73m. Rowley is legally blind. Paul English of Canada has run 1500m in 4:08.8, while J. Landos of Poland has a time of 50.7 in the 400m run. Both runners have 5 percent of normal vision.

Sightless Fritz Assmy of West Germany placed first in the 100m and 200m runs for his age group, 65–69, in the World Masters Games of 1979. His times were 12.5 and 26.0, to establish records for blind or sighted competitors. He runs with his sighted son-in-law. Legally blind Ivy Granstrom set records for her age group in the 1500m, 5000m, and 10,000m runs at the Canadian Masters Championships for sighted athletes in 1980.

Legally blind Elwin Kelsey of California and his partner placed fifth in the National Junior Pairs ice competition. This earned him an occupation skating in an ice show. Stash Serafin of Pennsylvania is an outstanding figure skater, though totally blind. He has been featured on national television. In 1980, legally blind Michael Lawson placed second in Alaska's Men's Solo Disco Roller Skating Meet. He finished eleventh in the West Regional Tournament. A blind man, Gordon Gund, is vice-president of the Minnesota North Stars professional ice hockey team.

Legally blind Kim Orsick as an 8th grade student competed in the 1978 National Women's Weightlifting Meet. She deadlifted 240 pounds and bench pressed 180 pounds.

In the 1979 New Mexico State Gymnastics Meet, legally blind Pita Quintana placed second in vaulting and fifth in all-around. Letters in gymnastics were recently won by Gail Castonquay at Weymouth South High School in Massachusetts and Anna McHale at Magnolia High School in Anaheim, California. In 1979, legally blind Don Bleloch bowled a 298 game. As everyone knows, 300 is perfect. Thousands of visually handicapped persons bowl. Jenny Reeves, a sightless bowler, rolled a three-game set of 454 at the 1965 International Bowling Congress Tournament. Although Charles Boswell of Alabama lost his vision in World War II, he regularly shoots golf in the low 90s. Once he made a hole-in-one on a 147-yard par 3 hole.

Over 350 blind teachers instruct sighted children in the public schools in our country. Sightless Bill Schmidt was a teacher and a principal, and recently became assistant superintendent of the Temple City Public Schools in California. During high school and college, he was an outstanding wrestler. Of his experience he says, "Wrestling helped in making many acquaintances. I also believe that through the sport I gained a degree of poise and self-confidence that benefitted me in later years. I feel that my team-mates and school-mates accepted me as an equal." As an avocation, Bill Schmidt has put automobile motors together. He has also built a cabin in the mountains. Schmidt believes that being blind is not a matter of having the lights turned out, but rather one of adjustment.

Chapter 2

ATTITUDES TOWARD BLINDNESS

To be able to help impaired individuals, the most important factors that able-bodied parents, educators, physical educators, recreators, and others must develop are positive attitudes toward disabled persons. To be comfortable with disabled persons, one must firmly believe in their capabilities. One who feels superior to impaired individuals, cannot have empathy with them. Most handicapped persons can detect lack of empathy and insincerity where it exists. If an able-bodied person is unable to feel comfortable with a handicapped individual, he may not be trying hard enough. If after a strong effort, negative attitudes still exist, perhaps an able-bodied person should come to realize that he will not be effective in teaching or helping a disabled individual.

By far the most important factor in successful mainstreaming of handicapped children in public schools is the presence of positive attitudes on the part of the teacher in a classroom. If the teacher is supportive of the handicapped child, the students will accept him. It is the responsibility of administrators to place impaired children in environments where positive attitudes exist. If positive attitudes do not exist, administrators should arrange for in-service training, with the hope of changing negative to positive attitudes. The most effective leader of such training is a qualified handicapped person.

What are some of the most important positive attitudes which need to be developed to successfully help handicapped persons? First, some positive attitudes toward all disabled persons will be discussed. The remainder of the chapter will be devoted to a discussion of attitudes toward blindness.

Attitudes toward Disabled Persons

The best philosophy which can be adopted toward handicapped individuals is to accent the positive and eliminate the negative, in thought and action. Stress should be given to ability, not disability; emphasis should be on potential, not deficiency, encouragement, rather than discouragement.

Nobody has the right to set limitations on another's potential. Do not treat an individual as he is, but rather treat him as he should or could be. Then he is much more likely to become what he should or could be.

A basic need for everyone is to achieve self-confidence and acceptance by his peers. This happens when some success is achieved. One cannot achieve success until given the opportunity to try. Once a child feels confidence in his accomplishments, a host of other things begin to fall into place.

Impaired individuals are basically people with the same needs and aspirations as their able-bodied peers. What is right and good for the able-bodied is, in most cases, also right and good for the disabled. Thus, if physical education is good for the able-bodied individual, it is good for the disabled person. The values of physical education which come to able-bodied individuals also come to impaired persons. If participation in physical education results in social, emotional, physical, and mental development of able-bodied individuals, then it is just as important, if not more so, for disabled persons.

Physical education can contribute to intellectual development by teaching what it means to compete, to strive, to achieve, and accept the agonies of defeat when it becomes necessary to do so. Physical education can teach community development through fair play and teamwork. Such concepts are important to all people, both the able-bodied and disabled. Thousands of years ago Hippocrates pointed out, "Activity strengthens—inactivity weakens." Disabled people have the right to become strong.

Mainstreaming means that impaired individuals are to be given opportunities to participate in the least restrictive and most productive environments. Those who can benefit from regular programs in schools and the community should be given the opportunity to participate in them. Some may need to develop abilitites in special programs before entering the mainstream. Whenever possible, disabled people should work and play with their able-bodied peers.

Disabled children have the right to grow up in a world where they are not treated differently. They have the right to be welcomed. They have the right to be given identical privileges and responsibilities. To become a productive, well-adjusted member of society, a person must learn the value and cultural patterns of his society.

Abilities Incorporated of New York has eloquently and pleadingly presented the inner feelings, true desires, and personal perceptions of impaired people in these words:

> "I do not choose to be a common man. It is my right to be uncommon—if I can. I seek opportunity—not security. I do not wish to be a kept citizen, humbled and dulled by having the state look after me. I want to take the calculated risk; to dream and to build, to fail and to succeed. I refuse to barter incentive for a dole. I prefer the challenge of life to the guaranteed existence; the thrill of fulfillment to the stale calm of Utopia. I will not trade freedom for beneficence nor my dignity for a handout. I will never cower before any master nor bend to any threat. It is my heritage to stand erect, proud and unafraid; to think and act for myself, enjoy the benefits of my creations, and to face the world boldly and say, this I have done."

Disabled persons want representation on governing bodies of agencies and organizations which offer services to them. The consumers of services definitely want an opportunity to have input in the decision-making process. Some laws have been passed to this effect (see Chapter 3).

Attitudes held by many educators and a large segment of the general public place many more limitations upon activities of the visually im-

paired than the actual loss of some or all vision. About two-thirds (over 18,000) of all visually handicapped children enrolled in public schools are excused from physical education or are being given watered-down courses. As adults, many blind persons must accept pensions or work in industries subsidized by the government. Helen Keller said, "The curse of the blind is not blindness, but idleness." Conditions are improving and more people are becoming enlightened. More blind people are being encouraged to work in regular industry and take part in sports.

Attitudes of Family and Public

The family is a mirror of society. Attitudes commonly held by the public are found in families of many visually impaired persons. For example, many parents shield their children from bumps and overprotect them in other ways. By making life unusually easy for their children, parents overlook the importance of firsthand experiences — including bumps and bruises — in the learning process. When a child is encouraged to be passive, the condition can negatively influence his total development, attitude, and drive in later years.

Some parents of blind children not only react negatively to a child's blindness but to the child as well. After the initial shock reaction, parents can very easily develop deep-seated guilt feelings. In attempting to overcome these feelings, they may overcompensate by becoming overprotective, which results in much idleness and lost opportunities to learn for the child. Still other parents completely ignore or reject their visually handicapped children.

A blind child who enters a classroom is, like any other child, a product of his environment. For a large percentage of blind children, the environment is different from that of their sighted classmates. Personal relationships of most visually handicapped children have been affected to some extent by people's reactions to their impairment. Of all handicapping conditions, blindness appears to arouse the strongest feelings of fear and anxiety. Blind persons live in a society which views blindness as a tragedy. Sighted people often equate blindness with death even though hundreds of thousands of visually handicapped people have learned to live with loss of vision. There still exist prevailing beliefs that blind people are helpless, unhappy, and impoverished. Too many blind people live in an environment where their capabilities are underestimated and untapped. Because of the influence of these attitudes, many of them do not realize their full potentialities. On the other hand, some people believe blind persons are geniuses with superior powers of sensory compensation — the sixth sense fallacy. Fortunately, realistic appraisal of blindness is very slowly becoming more common by the public.

These same prevailing attitudes are often found in public schools. Rather than openly express their basic fear of blindness, administrators and teachers frequently try to justify school policies by stating beliefs not based upon fact. Four such notions, all false, are:

Blind children have more accidents and injuries than those with normal vision.

Blind children are unable to participate effectively in regular or adapted physical education activities.

Blind children require more supervision from teachers than those with normal vision.

Blind children are shunned or not accepted by their classmates.

Unfortunately, these misconceptions often result in indefensible practices. For example, in physical education for blind students, such widespread practices include: excusing students altogether from the program;

giving unearned marks for playing table games; and allowing blind children to keep score for sighted classmates, give out towels, equipment, or other supplies, and take part in passive and unchallenging activities. In one school students received marks for merely standing outside the gym door day after day!

Accidents to blind children should be of no more concern than to other children. Thousands of sightless children have participated safely in vigorous physical education activities in residential schools for the blind for more than 100 years. More than 135 years ago Samuel Gridley Howe, a pioneer educator of the blind, said, "Do not too much regard bumps upon the forehead, rough scratches or bloody noses, even these may have their good influences. At the worst, they affect only the bark, and do not injure the system like the rust of inaction."

No credence can be given to the argument that blind children cannot participate effectively in vigorous physical activities. Genevie Dexter, a

consultant in physical education of the California State Department of Education, says, "From observation, informal reports, and the lack of statistical data, there is no evidence in California that blind children have any more accidents than their seeing peers." At present approximately 4,000 visually handicapped children are safely participating in vigorous physical education programs in public schools throughout the United States. The personnel in these schools have not found more accidents among blind children than among seeing boys and girls. The fact that thousands of other children remain idle, or relatively so, is because of lack of information about blindness and physical education by administrators, teachers, parents, and the public. It is hoped that this booklet will convince school personnel to take a positive, rather than a negative, approach toward blindness.

13

Attitudes of Teachers and Parents

A blind child in a physical education class need not necessarily require more supervision from the teacher. Many schools, including Indian Hills Junior High School, Shawnee Mission, Kansas, pair a blind child with a classmate with normal vision. The sighted children learn to give assistance only when required by their visually handicapped classmates. In the beginning, a sightless child must be shown to his locker, the activity area, and the shower. After a few days, he is usually able to get to class by himself. It may be necessary to assign key, rather than combination, locks to blind students.

During activity periods teachers demonstrate skills, movements, and patterns for the class. Teachers can use a blind child as a subject for the demonstrations. In this way he can get the feel of the movements. Otherwise, a sighted companion can pass on the necessary information to his visually handicapped classmate. A devoted teacher may wish to give a blind child brief instruction before or at the end of a class period. In any event, a blind or partially seeing child does not require much extra time from the teacher. Additional supervision is not the barrier to a child's participation in a physical education class — it is more likely to be the teacher's attitude toward blindness.

Some reading and careful thought can do much to change attitudes. Parents, educators, and recreation specialists who attempt to analyze honestly their reactions discover that negative feelings toward impairments, disabilities, and handicaps in general do not necessarily elicit a similar reaction to a visually handicapped child. When one looks beyond the condition, he finds that visually impaired boys and girls are much more like other children than they are different. Despite some limitations upon a child's sensory input, his abilities are very similar to those of his sighted peers. However, in some cases different methods must be used to accomplish the same goals.

Blindness is not a tragedy; rather it is a nuisance that can be compensated for or overcome. Parents and teachers should encourage and help blind children lead active lives among their sighted peers. They should honestly evaluate a visually handicapped child's abilities and allow him to try anything within reasonable reach. Every human being, including one who is blind, is entitled to the right to try, to fail, and to reach his full potential. One cannot develop or succeed if he is not given the opportunity to try. Teacher and parental attitudes should be based on the premise that a blind child is entitled to all of the rights and privileges that other children should have.

It is important for a teacher to let children know that he has confidence in them and their abilities. It is particularly desirable for a teacher to let those with handicapping conditions know that he expects good performances from them. Positive expectations tend to bring out the best in any child. A wise teacher emphasizes abilities, not disabilities; encourages, doesn't discourage; and accentuates the positive, not the negative.

Attitude Recently Changed to Law

Section 904 of the Education Act Amendments of 1972 states:

> No person in the United States shall on the ground of blindness or severely impaired vision be denied admission in any course of study by a recipient of Federal financial assistance for any education program or activity but nothing herein shall be construed to require any such institution to provide any special services to such person because of his blindness or visual impairment.

Under the law, visually handicapped individuals have the right to enroll in any course, including physical education, which is offered in school districts and colleges receiving financial assistance from the federal government. Finally, attitude has been changed to law.

Attitudes of Blind Persons toward Blindness

Attitudes of a blind person toward blindness are crucial in determining success or failure in life. His attitudes are determined by those closest to him, his parents and teachers. It has been said, "What you think of me, I'll think of me; what I think of me, will be me." Parents and teachers must obtain the truth about blindness so that healthy attitudes will develop.

If people have respect for, and confidence in, a blind individual he will more likely develop a positive self-image. He will view blindness as an impairment or disability which will not prevent him from living a happy, independent, and productive life. A blind person with this viewpoint can be educated and trained to his fullest potential.

If a blind person's philosophy toward his impairment is similar to that of the public's, he is more likely to feel inferior and may withdraw within himself. He may lack motivation to learn in school and to try in other aspects of life. He may feel the world owes him a living and therefore resort to begging. Government pensions are available to legally blind people; those who beg do so by choice. Blind beggars weaken the image which capable blind persons are trying so hard to improve. Some cities, such as Salt Lake City, Utah, do not allow blind beggars to remain in town.

Blindness as Ability, Not Disability

Attitudes of blind persons and others toward blindness are of utmost importance in determining success or failure in programs of education, recreation, and rehabilitation for visually handicapped individuals. Understanding blindness assists doubters to become positive thinkers and doers. Information on how to overcome blindness is available, and more people involved with blindness should make use of it.

Courtesy Suggestions

Here are some points of courtesy to make relationships more comfortable between blind and sighted individuals:

1. Please address me directly and not through my guide or companion.
2. I can walk more easily with you than with a dog or cane. But don't grab my arm or try to propel me; let me take yours. I'll keep a half step behind, to anticipate curbs and steps. Going down stairs I may prefer to hold a railing. When giving me directions, make it plain whether you mean your right or my right.
3. Speak to me when you enter the room and tell me who you are — don't play guessing games. Introduce me to the others, including children. Guide my hand to the arm or back of a chair.
4. For me, doors should be completely closed or wide open — a half-open door is a hazard; so are toys on the floor. Warn me of coffee tables and projecting lamp shades — I hate to break things.
5. At dinner time, tell me quietly how things are arranged. Perhaps my meat will be at six o'clock, peas at eleven o'clock, potatoes at two. And I may ask help in cutting my meat.
6. Don't avoid words like "See" — I use them too! I'm always glad to see you.
7. I don't want pity. But don't talk about the "wonderful compensations" of blindness — whatever I've learned has been by hard work.
8. I'll discuss blindness with you if you're curious, but it's an old story to me. I have as many other interests as you do.
9. If I'm your house guest, show me the bathroom, closet, dresser, window, and the outlet for my electric razor. The light switch, too; I like to know whether the lights are on.
10. Don't think of me as a blind man. I am a man who happens to be blind.

Chapter 3

MANDATES AND MISSIONS

Dr. *Julian Stein,*
Professor of Physical Education,
George Mason University,
Fairfax, Virginia

Federal legislative mandates have greatly influenced and positively affected opportunities for individuals with handicapping conditions to participate in physical education, recreation, and sport programs. Effects of three laws in particular are reviewed in this chapter:

- The Education for All Handicapped Children Act (P.L. 94-142);
- Section 504 of the Rehabilitation Act of 1973 (P.L. 93-112);
- Amateur Sports Act of 1978 (P.L. 95-606).

Each of these federal laws has had many indirect effects as well as direct influences on programs and activities involving persons with handicapping conditions. State laws and local codes have been developed and implemented to be in compliance with and follow requirements of federal mandates. As a result many new opportunities have been afforded individuals with handicapping conditions in both integrated (mainstreamed) and segregated settings. Because physical education, recreation, and/or sport have been specifically identified in these laws, there is greater attention to physical and motor needs as well as leisure-time pursuits of individuals with handicapping conditions. New recognition and greater importance have been given to running and recreation as supplements to the traditional 3R's!

The Education for All Handicapped Children Act (P.L. 94-142)

The Education for All Handicapped Children Act guarantees every child with a handicapping condition a free appropriate education conducted in the least restrictive environment and governed by a written individualized education program. The only curricular area specifically included in the definition of special education is physical education. Special education is defined as:

> "...specially designed instruction, at no cost to the parent, to meet the unique needs of a handicapped child, including classroom instruction, instruction in

17

physical education [*emphasis added*], *home instruc-*
tion, and instruction in hospitals and institutions."[1]
All stipulations and requirements for special education are required for
physical education which is defined as:

- development of physical and motor fitness;
- development of fundamental motor skills and patterns;
- development of skills in aquatics, dance, individual and group games
  and sports (including intramural sports).[2]

Intent and emphasis are clarified. Physical education has been included
in P.L. 94-142 of and for itself. This intent comes through loud and clear in
the wording of regulations providing administrative direction for implementing P.L. 94-142—instruction in physical education and development
of each of the delineated physical and motor areas. Congressional intent
and rationale for including and emphasizing physical education in P.L.
94-142 are stated in House of Representatives Report No. 94-332:

> "*The Committee expects the Commissioner of Educa-*
> *tion to take whatever action is necessary to assure that*
> *physical education services are available to all handi-*
> *capped children and has specifically included physical*
> *education within the definition of special education to*
> *make clear that the Committee expects such services,*
> *specially designed where necessary, to be provided as*
> *an integral part of the educational program of every*
> *handicapped child.*
>
> *Special education as set forth in the Committee bill*
> *includes instruction in physical education, which is*
> *provided as a matter of course to all nonhandicapped*
> *children enrolled in public elementary and secondary*
> *schools. The Committee is concerned that although*
> *these services are available to and required of all chil-*
> *dren in our school systems, they are often viewed as a*
> *luxury for handicapped children.*"[3]

Use of physical and motor activities is to be encouraged as a method or
approach to attain goals and objectives in cognitive (mental) and affective
(emotional and social) domains, but not at the expense of or by compromis-
ing the psychomotor (physical and motor) domain. To do differently would
be contrary to the intent and letter of the law.

Recreation is one of many related services which can be provided to
students with handicapping conditions if necessary for the individual to
benefit from primary special education services. Other areas specifically
included as related services are most all therapies—physical, occupa-

---

[1]"Education of Handicapped Children: Implementation of Part B of the Education of the
Handicapped Act." *Federal Register*, August 23, 1977, p. 42480.

[2]Ibid., p. 42480.

[3]*House of Representatives Report No. 94-332.* Washington, DC: U.S. House of Representatives.

18

tional, music, art, and dance.[4] It should be noted that by both definitions and interpretation, related services such as physical and occupational therapies cannot replace or supplant physical education. Such therapies are adjuncts to physical education, not the other way around. Within this context recreation is defined as:

- assessment of leisure function;
- therapeutic recreation services;
- recreation programs in schools and community agencies;
- leisure education.[5]

Recreation services can be included in a child's individualized education program and provided if needed for the individual to benefit from primary special education services. Recent court decisions in Massachusetts have resulted in recreation programming being required on individualized education programs so that specific needs could be met by severely or profoundly mentally retarded or multiply-handicapped students. Court decisions in Pennsylvania have required that programs for some severely or profoundly mentally retarded and multiply-involved students be provided during summer months despite the fact that this exceeds mandated requirements for students without handicapping conditions. These cases have many implications and potential applications for students with visual impairments. Visual impairments under P.L. 94-142 are defined as follows:

> *"Visually handicapped means a visual impairment which, even with correction, adversely affects a child's educational performance. The term includes both partially seeing and blind children."*[6]

Because an individual meets the criterion for blind or partially-sighted does not automatically qualify him for services under this law. Two criteria must be met for an individual to be considered handicapped under P.L. 94-142:

- Possess an identifiable handicapping condition as found in traditional categorical definitions;
- Have needs that require special education with or without related services. In terms of physical and motor areas this has been interpreted to mean students with needs that are of such a nature that they require long-term goals and short-term instructional objectives substantially different from those for students in regular physical education programs.[7]

---

[4]"Education of Handicapped Children: Implementation of Part B of the Education of the Handicapped Act." *Federal Register*, August 23, 1977, p. 42479.
[5]Ibid., p. 42479
[6]Ibid., p. 42479.
[7]Ibid., p. 42481.

To be considered handicapped and eligible for services under The Education for All Handicapped Children Act, a student must meet both of these criteria. Of course, it must be determined if each student with a handicapping condition has special needs or not. In the physical and motor areas this is approached in terms of individual student needs with respect to needs of other students of similar age. Special needs are those that are sufficiently different from needs of peers and classmates to require special attention of some type—different placements, modified activities, individualized methods, reduced teacher-pupil ratios, adaptive devices, special attention to class organization, peer tutoring, and adapted rules. For students with this type of special physical and motor needs, all stipulations of and requirements for individualized education programs must be satisfied including:

- statement of the child's present levels of educational performance;
- statement of annual goals including short-term instructional objectives;
- statement of specific special education and related services to be provided to the child and the extent to which the child will be able to participate in regular educational programs;
- projected dates for initiation of services and anticipated duration of services;
- appropriate objective criteria and evaluation procedures and schedules for determining on at least an annual basis whether short-term instructional objectives are being achieved.[8]

Many students with handicapping conditions, including some who are blind or partially sighted, can be safely, successfully, and with personal satisfaction, integrated into regular physical education, community recreation, and interscholastic sport programs with appropriate accommodations. Such accommodations, not considered special needs in the sense just discussed, are not only expected but required to be included in each student's individualized education program. This requirement is clearly manifested in a position paper on individualized education programs which appeared in the *Federal Register* of January 19, 1981. Specifications of this position paper, now considered part of official rules and regulations for P.L. 94-142, include different physical education program arrangements and extensive physical education must be described or referred to in an individualized education program (IEP):

- *Regular physical education with non-handicapped students.* If a handicapped student can fully participate in the regular physical education program without any special modifications to compensate for the student's handicap, it would not be necessary to describe or refer to physical education in the IEP. On the other hand, if some modifications to the regular physical education program are necessary for the student to be able to participate in that program, those modifications must be described in the IEP.

---

[8]Ibid., p. 42491.

- *Specially-designed physical education.* If a handicapped student needs a specially-designed physical education program, that program must be addressed in all applicable areas of the IEP, e.g., present levels of educational performance, goals and objectives, and services to be provided. However, these statements would not have to be presented in any more detail than other special education services included in a student's IEP.
- *Physical education in separate facilities.* If a handicapped student is educated in a separate facility, the physical education program for that student must be described or referred to in the IEP. However, the kind and amount of information to be included in the IEP would depend on the physical-motor needs of the student and type of physical education program that is to be provided.

Thus, if a student is in a separate facility that has a standard physical education program, e.g., a residential school for the deaf, and if it is determined on the basis of the student's most recent evaluation that the student is able to participate in that program without any modifications, then the IEP need only note such participation. On the other hand, if special modifications to the physical education program are needed for the student to participate, those modifications must be described in the IEP. Moreover, if the student needs an individually-designed physical education program, that program must be addressed under all applicable parts of the IEP.[9]

Representations of accommodations which are being made so that visually impaired students can participate in physical education, recreation, and sports programs include:

- buddy systems, peer tutoring, and student aides;
- adaptive devices such as beeper balls, bowling rails, and photoelectric cell archery sights or aimers;
- auditory and tactile input during instructional programs and coaching sessions;
- modified rules, adapted methods, and organizational patterns for classes which make it possible for the individual student to learn physical and motor skills and participate in physical education, recreation, and sport activities.

If a student has no special physical and motor needs and does not require accommodations, only the indications of no special physical and motor needs is to be included in the individualized education program. However, such determinations must be based on appropriate and adequate assessments—observations and informal techniques as well as results from norm- and criterion-referenced tests.

Only a child's parent(s), teacher(s), and someone certified to supervise special education (usually the building administrator or his designee) are required to participate in individualized education program meetings.

---

[9]"Assistance to States for Education of Handicapped Children: Interpretation of the Individualized Education Program (IEP)." *Federal Register*, January 19, 1981, p. 5471.

Physical educators and/or others knowledgeable of and conversant in assessing and interpreting motor behavior are not required to participate in individualized education program meetings. Therefore, professionals from these disciplines must volunteer such information; they are available to assist, and exercise professional initiative in the best interests of every child with a handicapping condition. Conversely, members of the individualized education program committee must seek information and recommendations from physical educators and involve them in planning meetings. It should be noted that this process is mandated in some states by laws which can exceed federal requirements.

Part of the individualized education program planning process is determining the appropriate, least restrictive environment for each child. Placement decisions are not done categorically or according to the type and severity of a child's handicapping condition. Placement decisions are individually made with respect to each child's abilities and disabilities, strengths and weaknesses, in relation to activities in the program. Therefore, a child could be integrated for some physical education activities and segregated for others. Such placement information is to be included in the individualized education program based on decisions by the committee.

Many misconceptions exist about the concept of least restrictive environment. Mainstreaming is a term commonly used for least restrictive environment. Various terms are used in different parts of the world to describe the goal and process of mainstreaming. Included among these diverse descriptive terms are normalization, least restrictive environment, zero reject principle, program accessibility, most normal setting feasible, most integrated setting possible, and integration. Implications of mainstreaming for teachers, leaders, and coaches involved in physical education, recreation, and sport programs are great. There is no intent when implementing mainstreaming principles and procedures to place every individual with a handicapping condition in regular programs and activities any more than special and segregated programs and activities are to be done away with for these populations! Key considerations are in determining needs and interests, abilities and disabilities, strengths and weaknesses, of each participant as an individual. Then placement decisions—integrated, segregated, some step between, or various combinations—are based upon the individual needs of each participant. Such needs are identified in terms of physical proficiency, motor ability, and requisite skills for safe, successful, and personally-satisfying participation in various physical education, recreation, and sport activities, not medical diagnosis.

Both the term and concept of mainstreaming continue to be misunderstood, inappropriately defined, and incorrectly applied. Within the context of this chapter mainstreaming refers to:

> ". . . appropriate education, physical education, recreation, and sport services and activities to individuals with handicapping conditions, regardless of levels of involvement, in settings as near to traditional practice as possible."

As such this definition does not:

> ". . . *suggest massive return to or placement of all children with learning problems in regular classes;*
> . . . *refer to separate settings as equivalent placement; or*
> . . . *mean the end of all self-contained special classes as service vehicles for children.*"

This definition does suggest:

> ". . . *a continuum of service alternatives appropriate to allow placement of children as individuals, not members of categories;*
> . . . *some system other than the dichotomy of either placement in regular classes or placement in special class;*
> . . . *need to integrate all levels of children with handicapping conditions to maximum extents possible;*
> . . . *need for greater understanding of children with handicapping conditions by all school personnel;*
> . . . *placement of children with handicapping conditions in their home districts whenever possible to insure home and school common peer relationships;*
> . . . *preventive services to children with potential learning problems as important, if not more so, than interventive services to children who have already demonstrated their learning handicap(s); and*
> . . . *new roles for educational personnel in providing services to individuals with handicapping conditions.*"[10]

The section in the rules and regulation on continuum of alternative education placements emphasizes these points:

- each public agency shall ensure that a continuum of alternative placements is available to meet the needs of handicapped children for special education and related services;
- include alternative placements such as instruction in regular classes, special classes, special schools, home instruction, and instruction in hospitals and institutions;
- make provision for supplementary services, such as resource room or itinerant instruction, to be provided in conjunction with regular class placements.[11]

---

[10]Coons, Dale E. "Mainstreaming Defined." IRUC Briefings I: 3(5).

[11]"Education of Handicapped Children: Implementation of Part B of the Education of the Handicapped Act." *Federal Register*, August 23, 1977, p. 42497.

Both parents, or the student himself (if over eighteen years of age) and local education agency are afforded protection by due process provisions of the law including:

- opportunity to examine records;
- independent educational evaluations;
- prior notice and parental consent;
- due process hearings with impartial hearing officers;
- opportunity to appeal decisions through impartial administrative reviews;
- right to civil actions;
- representation by surrogate parents.[12]

During the pendency of an administrative or judicial proceeding regarding a complaint, unless the public agency and parents of the child agree otherwise, the child involved in the complaint must remain in his present educational placement. If the complaint involves an application for initial admission to public school, the child, with consent of the parents, must be placed in the public school program until completion of all proceedings.

Seventy-five percent of all funds coming into states pass through state education agencies to local education agencies. Amounts received by states are based on a formula involving the number of children with handicapping conditions and the average amount spent on educating all students. Each state develops its criteria and procedures for distributing and making funds available to local education agencies. States can also receive additional funds through early childhood incentive provisions.

Although many people still look upon and consider P.L. 94–142 as a Bill of Rights or Civil Rights Act for persons with handicapping conditions, it is incorrect perception. The Education for All Handicapped Children Act is a formula grant program to assist state and local education agencies with excess costs incurred in educating students with handicapping conditions. State and local education agencies are required to support education of students with handicapping conditions to the same degrees and from the same sources as for students without handicapping conditions. P.L. 94–142 funds are then used for extra services and additional resources necessary to meet the needs of students with handiicapping conditions. Services and resources must be provided on bases of need, not availability. In addition, P.L. 94–142 funds cannot be used to supplant or replace state and/or local funds used in providing special education and related services to students with handicapping conditions.

Section 504 of the Rehabilitation Act (P.L. 93–112)

Section 504 of the Rehabilitation Act is civil rights legislation. It prohibits exclusion of, denial of benefits for, and discrimination against, individuals with handicapping conditions. This protects citizens with handicapping conditions in the same ways Title VI of the Civil Rights Act

---

[12]Ibid., p. 42495.

(1964) prohibits discrimination based on race, creed, color, or national origin, and Title IX of the Education Amendments (1971) prohibits discrimination based on sex. Section 504 simply states:

> ". . . no otherwise qualified handicapped individual in the United States shall, solely by reason of his handicap, be excluded from the participation in, be denied the benefits of, or be subjected to discrimination under any program or activity receiving Federal financial assistance."[13]

The protection and scope of Section 504 are broader and more comprehensive than P.L. 94–142. In addition to elementary and secondary school programs, provisions include protection against discrimination based on handicapping condition in:

- employment;
- preschool education;
- post-secondary education;
- health, welfare, and social services.

All programs sponsored or conducted by recipients of federal financial assistance are governed by Section 504, not just specific programs benefitting from such support. It should be noted that this principle has been unsuccessfully challenged in courts on several occasions. However, recent court judgments in Michigan and Virginia in Title IX cases have resulted in rulings delimiting compliance only to programs directly benefitting from federal financial assistance. Since all of the civil right mandates are worded and have been interpreted similarly, potential implications of these latest Title IX rulings for Section 504 are obvious and ominous. Federal financial assistance is not only direct monetary support but includes contributions such as:

> ". . . funds;
> . . . services of federal personnel; or
> . . . real and personal property or any interest in or use of such property, including transfers or leases of such property for less than fair market value or for reduced consideration, and proceeds from a subsequent transfer or lease of such property if the federal share of its fair market value is not returned to the federal government."[14]

Since virtually all cities, counties, and communities receive federal financial assistance, all programs administered and conducted by their parks and recreation departments must not be discriminatory; they must be accessible to all with handicapping conditions under current interpretations and applications of Section 504.

---

[13]"Non-discrimination on the Basis of Handicap in Programs and Activities Receiving or Benefitting from Federal Financial Assistance." *Federal Register*, May 4, 1977, p. 22676.

[14]Ibid., p. 22679.

Definition of populations covered and protected by Section 504 are broader than in P.L. 94–142. Handicapped person as defined in Section 504 means:

> "... any person who (a) has a physical or mental impairment which substantially limits one or more major life activities; (b) has a record of such an impairment; or (c) is regarded as having such an impairment."

Each of the three parts of this definition are clarified in the rules and regulations:

- "Physical or mental impairment means (a) any physiological disorder or condition, cosmetic disfigurement, or anatomical loss affecting one or more of the body systems; or (b) any mental or psychological disorder, such as mental retardation, organic brain syndrome, emotional or mental illness, and specific learning disabilities.
- Major life activities means functions such as caring for one's self, performing manual tasks, walking, seeing, hearing, speaking, breathing, learning, and working.
- Has a record of such an impairment means has a history of, or has been misclassified as having, a mental or physical impairment that substantially limits one or more major life activities.
- Is regarded as having an impairment means (a) has a physical or mental impairment that does not substantially limit major life activities but is treated by a recipient as constituting such a limitation; (b) has a physical or mental impairment that substantially limits major life activities only as a result of the attitudes of others toward such impairment; or (c) has none of the defined impairments but is treated by a recipient as having such an impairment."[15]

The principle of program accessibility is basic to Section 504. The intent of program accessibility is to guarantee individuals with handicapping conditions equal opportunities as those individuals having no handicapping conditions. Equality of opportunity and equal treatment are not synonymous terms. In fact, equal treatment can in and of itself be discriminatory!

Program accessibility is a way in which equal opportunity can be attained in programs and activities by individuals with handicapping conditions and able-bodied persons. Making facilities physically accessible is one way in which programs, employment as well as educational and recreational, can become accessible. So often architects and other professional providers of services responsible for planning facilities and implementing programs see things in much more complex and sophisticated ways than participants for whom such facilities and programs are designed

---

[15]Ibid., p. 22680.

want and need. This is as true for physical education, recreation, and sport facilities and activities as well as other program areas.

It is imperative to involve individuals with handicapping conditions in planning and at decision-and policy-making levels for programs and activities that so intimately affect them and so directly influence their futures and destinies. Representative of some ways in which physical education, recreation, and sport programs and activities can be made accessible for visually impaired persons are:

- use adaptive devices such as beeper balls for ball games, guide rails for bowling, and sound-sighting devices for archery;
- use buddy systems, peer tutoring, and student leaders to assist in learning and participating in movement patterns, motor skills, and sport activities;
- preteach skills and activities so that these students are aware of them before they are introduced in formal class settings;
- fully use auditory and tactile senses in presenting skills and activities so that emphasis is on strengths and functioning parts, not weaknesses and deficiencies.

Specific interpretations and applications of Section 504 relate to competitive sport programs—intramural, extramural, club, interscholastic, and intercollegiate. Individuals cannot be denied opportunities to participate in sport activities, including contact sports, because of handicapping conditions. For example, an individual cannot be denied opportunities to compete in sport activities because he possesses only one of paired body parts, e.g., limbs, eyes, or organs such as kidneys. While coaches, teachers, and other leaders have the responsibility to alert these individuals and their parents or guardians to potential consequences of injury to a remaining body part, the final decision to participate or not remains with the individual. This position has been affirmed and reaffirmed by official policy interpretation statements by the Office of Civil Rights and several court cases over the past ten years.[16]

Changes have also been made in both governance and playing rules to accommodate athletes with handicapping conditions. For example, the National Federation of State High School Associations, the governing body for high school sports, has made the following provisions that enable blind athletes to compete equitably in track and wrestling:

- Sighted partners or teammates can assist blind runners in distance events in track, cross-country, and marathon running so long as they are identified to meet management and other competitors and do not interfere with other athletes. Various types of contact are also permitted

---

[16]"Implications of Section 504 of the Rehabilitation Act as Related to Physical Education Instructional, Personnel Preparation, Intramural, and Interscholastic/Intercollegiate Programs." *Practical Pointers* 3:11. Washington, DC: The American Alliance for Health, Physical Education, Recreation and Dance.

including physical contact, verbal assistance, and use of short pieces of rope. Experiments are now being conducted with radio control through earphones to assist blind runners to compete more independently at higher levels of competition.[17]

- Sighted wrestlers are prohibited from gaining unfair advantages over blind opponents by moving behind them in the standing position. Sighted wrestlers must also go through with an attempted take down when it is started. To lock or not in the standing position becomes the choice of the two wrestlers just as in competition between two sighted wrestlers.[18]

Provisions of Section 504 also apply to personnel preparation programs and in leadership positions such as teaching and coaching. Again, an otherwise qualified individual cannot be denied admission to a professional preparation program or excluded from job consideration because of a handicapping condition. Schools, including colleges and universities, and employers are expected and required to make necessary, appropriate, and reasonable accommodations so that the student or employee is not denied such opportunities because of a handicapping condition. Representative of such accommodations are:

- Make facilities used by employees readily accessible to and usable by handicapped persons.[19]
- Restructure jobs, use part-time or modified work schedules, acquire or modify equipment or devices, provide readers or interpreters, and other similar actions.[20]
- Redesign equipment; reassign classes or other services to accessible buildings; assign aides to beneficiaries; use home visits; deliver health, welfare, or other social services at alternate accessible sites; alter existing facilities; construct new facilities; or introduce any other methods that result in making programs or activities accessible to handicapped persons.[21]

A recipient is not required to make structural changes in existing facilities where other methods are effective in achieving compliance. In choosing among available methods for meeting requirements, give priority to those methods that offer programs and activities to handicapped persons in the most integrated setting appropriate.

A number of totally blind individuals have been successful teachers and school administrators. At least two public high school physical education

---

[17]*Track and Field Rulebook.* Elgin, IL: National Federation of State High School Associations, annually.

[18]*Wrestling Rulebook.* Elgin, IL: National Federation of State High School Associations, annually.

[19]"Non-discrimination on the Basis of Handicap in Programs and Activities Receiving or Benefitting from Federal Financial Assistance." *Federal Register,* May 4, 1977, p. 22681.

[20]Ibid., p. 22681.

[21]Ibid., p. 22685.

teachers have been blind and have also successfully coached interscholastic wrestling teams. Others have attained such specialized certifications as
American Red Cross Water Safety Instructor.

Amateur Sports Act of 1978 (P.L. 95–606)

The Amateur Sports Act of 1978 was enacted by Congress to reorganize
the United States Olympic Committee:

> ". . . to promote and coordinate amateur athletic activ-
> ity in the United States, to recognize certain rights for
> United States amateur athletes, to provide for the reso-
> lution of disputes involving national governing bodies,
> and for other purposes."[22]

Among specific objectives and purposes of the U.S. Olympic Committee
are to:

> ". . . encourage and provide assistance to amateur ath-
> letic programs and competition for handicapped indi-
> viduals, including, where feasible, expansion of oppor-
> tunities for meaningful participation by handicapped
> individuals in programs of athletic competition for
> able-bodied individuals."[23]

The United States Olympic Committee, therefore, established a Handicapped in Sports Committee consisting of sixteen persons. Included on this
committee are two representatives from each of the following organizations:

- Amateur Athletic Association for the Deaf;
- National Association of Sports for Cerebral Palsy;
- National Wheelchair Athletic Association;
- Special Olympics;
- United States Association for Blind Athletes.

One representative from each of these organizations on the Handicapped
in Sports Committee must be an athlete who has been an active competitor
within the immediate past ten years. This obviously means that at least one
of these organizational representatives must be an individual with a handicapping condition. This requirement fosters and furthers self-advocacy for
individuals with handicapping conditions and among athletes themselves
as emphasized by U.S.O.C. in complying with the Amateur Sports Act. The
other six members of the Handicapped in Sports Committee are appointed
at large by the U.S.O.C.

Provisions for National Governing Bodies are included in P. L. 95–606.
Only one National Governing Body for each sport included on programs of
Olympic or Pan American Games can be recognized by the U.S.O.C. Asso-
ciations governing sports for athletes with handicapping conditions do not

---

[22]*Amateur Sports Act of 1978.* Washington, DC: 95th Congress, November 8, 1978 (92 Stat
3045–3058), p. 3045.

[23]Ibid., p. 3046.

meet criteria so they cannot qualify as National Governing Bodies. However these associations do qualify for Type E membership in the U.S.O.C. and can affiliate with specific National Governing Bodies. For example, the National Wheelchair Basketball Association is affiliated with the United States of America Basketball Association and the United States Association for Blind Athletes with the Track Athletic Congress.

Type E member organizations are eligible to receive some financial support from U.S.O.C. and participate as members of its governance body. During 1981 each of the associations represented on the U.S.O.C. Handicapped in Sports Committee received $50,000 for use in program development and support of athletes preparing for international competition. These funds were provided as a one-time allocation to assist these associations in planning, implementing, and furthering both their developmental and competitive programs.

Each National Governing Body must demonstrate, that its . . . board of directors or other such governing board includes among its voting members individuals who are actively engaged in amateur athletic competition in the sport for which recognition is sought or who have represented the United States in international amateur athletic competition in the sport for which recognition is sought within the preceding ten years, and that the membership and voting power held by such individuals is not less than twenty percent of such membership, and voting power held in that board of directors or other such governing board.

The ten-year-twenty percent stipulations for National Governing Bodies have been incorporated into the U.S.O.C. Constitution (Article XVI, Section 2) and apply to all standing committees. Therefore, by U.S.O.C. constitutional provisions, the Handicapped in Sports Committee must be at least twenty percent athletes who have actively competed within the preceding ten years.

Another responsibility of a national governing body for the sport it governs is to:

> ". . . encourage and support research, development,
> and dissemination of information in the areas of sports
> medicine and sports safety."[24]

As a first step in accomplishing this goal in relation to sports for individuals with handicapping conditions, a meeting in March 1978 was devoted to sports medicine issues and concerns for athletes with handicapping conditions. Definite courses of action were charted in which publications handling priority concerns were planned. Other activities discussed included specific training and inservice activities for personnel involved in sport programs involving athletes with handicapping conditions.

Summary

The direction and thrust of P.L. 94–142, Section 504 of P.L. 93–112, and P.L. 95–606, are clear. Individuals with handicapping conditions are

---

[24]Ibid., p. 3053.

guaranteed equal opportunities in physical education, recreation, and sport programs and activities. These guarantees apply at all levels—local, state, regional, national, and international. Responsibilities of professional providers of services, physical education teachers, recreation specialists, coaches, administrators, therapists, *ad infinitum*, are also clear. Services are to be based on need, not availability. It is the responsibility of teachers, leaders, and coaches to make the necessary accommodations so that individuals with handicapping conditions, including those who are blind and partially sighted, can participate safely, successfully, and with personal satisfaction in physical education, recreation, and sport activities.

Segregation and separation from the mainstream of society can be justified *only* if an individual's physical and motor needs are of such a nature that they cannot be met in regular settings. When special needs in these areas are present, all provisions of the individualized education program apply.

Equality of opportunity extends to extracurricular activities including intramural and extramural clubs, and interscholastic and intercollegiate sports. Several court cases have affirmed rights of individuals with only one eye to participate in both interscholastic and intercollegiate sports, including those of a contact nature. Increased opportunities at international levels along with greater coordination within and among governance organizations for special sports have been fostered and stimulated by provisions of the Amateur Sport Act. Under this legislation the United States Olympic Committee has established a Handicapped in Sport Committee to promote and coordinate programs for which U.S.O.C. is responsible.

Despite outstanding legislative support during the 1970s, many factors cloud issues and the future beyond the early 1980s, e.g., financial cutbacks, budget reductions, recisions, deregulation, repeal, and other processes that have been introduced at various times in recent months by President Ronald Reagan, his administration, and various members of Congress.

Concerted efforts by many concerned and dedicated individuals have thus far thwarted these attacks. However, the battles are not over. Political astuteness has been a trademark and characteristic of this administration. For this reason ongoing monitoring of administrative, legislative, and judicial rulings and actions is a must. Contacts of all types—letters, telegrams, telephone calls, personal visits—must be made about each and every issue and concern. Only with coordinated efforts of many concerned individuals has each of these laws become a reality. It will take the same efforts by as many or more individuals so that gains painstakingly attained can be maintained and continued progress assured.

References

"Individualized Education Programs." *Practical Pointer* 1:6. Washington, DC: The American Alliance for Health, Physical Education, Recreation and Dance.

"Individualized Education Programs: Assessment and Evaluation in Physical Education." *Practical Pointer* 1:9. Washington, DC: The American Alliance for Health, Physical Education, Recreation and Dance.

"Individualized Education Programs: Methods for Individualizing Physical Education." *Practical Pointer* 1:7. Washington, DC: The American Alliance for Health, Physical Education, Recreation and Dance.

"Questions and Answers on P.L. 94-142 and Section 504." *AAHPERD Update,* Reston, VA: The American Alliance for Health, Physical Education, Recreation and Dance. (These columns have appeared regularly since September, 1977.)

Stein, Julian U. "The Mission and the Mandate: New Challenges for Physical Education under P.L. 94-142 and Section 504." *Amicus,* March/April, 1978.

"Tips on Mainstreaming: Do's and Don'ts in Activity Programs." *Practical Pointer* 1: 10. Washington, DC: The American Alliance for Health, Physical Education, Recreation and Dance.

United States Olympic Committee Constitution. Colorado Springs, CO: United States Olympic Committee.

Chapter 4

FACTS ABOUT BLINDNESS

What Is Blindness?

Definitions of blindness range from complete loss of sight to varying degrees of residual vision. The most commonly accepted definition of blindness is "central visual acuity no greater than 20/200 in the better eye with correction." The term 20/200 means that a visually handicapped individual sees at 20 feet what a person with normal vision sees at 200 feet. This is known as legal blindness, and makes one eligible for public assistance and income tax deduction. Most people with vision below 20/200 have some useful vision, if only ability to distinguish between light and dark. Others can follow sidewalks as they walk and sometimes see red and green traffic lights. Still others, can read large type or regular type with magnifying glasses. For most educational purposes, the standard of 20/200 is used to define a blind child. Such a child usually uses Braille, but he may read large print and be enrolled in a sight utilization class.

Many public schools have classes for partially sighted youngsters with visual acuity between 20/200 and 20/70. Partially sighted children may use large print or read regular type with magnifying glasses. Some can read regular print without glasses of any kind if the lighting is proper.

The American Foundation for the Blind prefers that the term "blindness" be reserved for a complete loss of sight, with all other degrees of visual loss considered as visual impairments. This definition is the most meaningful for physical educators and recreation personnel, particularly if *visual impairment* and *partially sighted* are used interchangeably.

It is estimated that there are half a million legally blind people in the United States. There is wide variation in the age of the onset of blindness. Some individuals have no memory of what things look like; others become blind at various times during childhood, after becoming established in a vocation, or during later years. Studies indicate that blindness is largely a problem of old age—about three-fourths of the blind are over 40 years of age, and 3/5 have reached the age of 60 before losing their vision. Over 36,000 children read Braille or large type books from the American Printing House for the Blind. About 80%, or over 28,000 children attend public schools, while the rest are in residential schools for the blind.

Vision is a blessing, even if possessed for only a short time. Children who lose their vision after 5 or 6 years of age do not have as much difficulty adjusting to physical and recreational activities as those blind from early childhood. The age at which vision is lost definitely influences one's mental outlook. The onset of blindness means one thing to a child and something else in later years.

Causes of Blindness

The most common causes of blindness are diseases, heredity, and accidents. To be more specific, cataracts, atrophy of the optic nerve, glaucoma, venereal disease, and diabetes, cause much blindness. It is estimated that 35,000 people lose their vision each year, and that one-half this number could be prevented.

Physical educators and recreation personnel should know that only a very small percentage of visually handicapped students have eye conditions which might be endangered by vigorous activity. Extensive experience of personnel in residential schools for the blind shows that only a very small percentage of students has had to be assigned light activities. Of course, school personnel must check eye reports and student records before permitting vigorous activity.

Only a few articles on sports and vision have been written by ophthalmologists. One article by Dr. Griffin Allen of Cleveland has pointed out that schools which do not permit visually handicapped children to take part in physical education, usually increase, not decrease, problems for these youngsters. He has found that not nearly as many restrictions had to be placed on the activities of myopic children as was once thought necessary. They can safely dive into water or fall or be thrown to the mat or turf. Resulting jars are distributed over the entire body, so no undue stress is placed on the eye and there is little likelihood that a retina will detach. Should a retina be torn loose, the chances are very good today that it can be reattached so that normal visual functions can continue. Precautions should be taken to prevent direct blows to the eye by fingers, elbows, or small balls.

Sometimes students get so much correction from glasses that their performance in vigorous athletics is markedly decreased when the glasses are removed. Such children should be provided with special plastic or case-hardened safety lens to withstand rugged treatment. If the parents cannot afford such glasses, the physical educator might contact the PTA or local service club to obtain the necessary funds.

Ophthalmologists and physical educators need to exchange information. Physicians have a responsibility to inform themselves about goals and activities of physical education programs for visually handicapped children. Informed physicians will encourage blind children to participate in vigorous physical education activities, except in those few cases where physical conditions do not permit.

Aids for Blind and Visually Impaired People

Many people with residual vision are able to read, using such optical aids as hand magnifying glasses or heavy spectacles. Today there are low vision clinics in almost every large metropolitan area.

Students in classes for the visually impaired use various devices to aid in their reading and mathematics. They make use of such aids as tapes, recordings, talking clocks, and talking calculators. The optacon is a reading device which turns print into raised dots which are in shapes of printed letters. Much practice is required to attain enough speed to make reading in this manner worthwhile. The newest reading machine turns print into the spoken word. This device promises to be widely used when the cost of production can be reduced. For people who have low vision, reading machines somewhat similar to television sets enlarge print a great many times and make it possible to read regular print. These television reading machines are commonly found in classes for the visually impaired and some public libraries.

Many aids are helpful to the blind in the shop, kitchen, and around the house. A local agency for the blind will give information on aids of this type.

Braille is a system of dots read by the fingers. Much Braille material is furnished to blind individuals free of charge. Talking books, long playing records, and, more recently, books recorded on magnetic tape make available much more reading material for visually handicapped persons. Books, magazines, and at least one newspaper and one national magazine are now printed in large type by commercial firms and some organizations for the blind. All of these aids can be borrowed from libraries for the blind located throughout the country. Special education instruction materials centers at the American Printing House for the Blind (1839 Frankfort Avenue, Louisville, KY 40206) and at Michigan State University (USOE/MSU IMC for handicapped children and youth, 213 Erickson Hall, Michigan State University, East Lansing, MI 48823) have special collections and services available for personnel working with visually handicapped individuals and groups. The Association for the Education of the Visually Handicapped, commonly known as AEVH, and the American Association of Workers for the Blind, commonly known as AAWB, (206 North Washington Street, Alexandria, VA 22314) are sources of much information on blindness.

A small percentage of sightless people travel with guide dogs. Many use canes or walk with sighted companions. Most electronic devices designed to assist blind persons to travel are not commonly used because of great expense or lack of perfection.

Blind People Are Not Amazing

Blind persons are not amazing; rather, they make use of their remaining senses better than most people. A blind person does not have acute hearing automatically. Since he depends on sound cues to get information, he pays more attention to sound than most sighted people.

Blind people can handle one, five, and ten dollar bills, even if they cannot see the numbers. When told by a sighted person what each denomination is, they fold each bill a certain way, according to its denomination. Recently, when the Federal government tried to devise a system to help blind people identify bills, one blind man expressed the thoughts of many in saying, "Blind people need an opportunity to earn money. Once they get it, they can usually find a way to handle it."

A sightless person cannot tell color by touch. In dealing with clothes, he will ask a sighted companion to tell him colors of socks. He then places red

35

1980 Olympic goal ball.

pairs in one corner of the drawer, blue in another, orange in another, and black in still another. A guide dog cannot distinguish colors either; he and his master work together through traffic sounds when travelling.

Acts of blind people which appear amazing to some people are simply a matter of common sense. Information is obtained through touch and sound cues which have no importance to those who have sight.

Chapter 5

EDUCATING VISUALLY HANDICAPPED CHILDREN

In the United States, two basic approaches are used to educate visually impaired children: (1) residential facilities, and (2) special classes and integration into regular classes in public schools. Residential schools have conducted education programs for visually impaired children since 1832. Formal classes for blind and partially seeing pupils were introduced in the public schools of our country about 80 years ago. Until World War II, only 10 percent of legally blind students attended special classes in public schools. Since that time, sweeping changes have taken place in educational programs for visually handicapped children. Today about 80 percent or 28,000 blind and partially seeing pupils attend special classes or are integrated into public schools. The percentage varies from state to state. For example, in California about 96 percent of blind and partially seeing students receive their education in public schools, while in the southeastern states from 10 to 20 percent are educated in this manner.

There are advantages and disadvantages to each system of education. In residential schools, boys and girls are likely to miss many contacts with sighted children unless the personnel organize extensive programs for this purpose. Most residential schools have adequate programs of instruction in mobility, physical education, industrial arts, homemaking and daily living skills. Some public schools now have adequate programs in all of these areas, but many schools lack one or more such programs. However, more and more public schools are accepting their responsibility to offer complete educational programs to visually impaired students.

Whether a visually handicapped child should attend his local public school or go to a state residential school depends upon a number of factors. In fact, it might be desirable to educate a boy or girl in one system during a certain period of his life and then change to the other system.

Purposes of educating boys and girls do not differ whether or not they are impaired, disabled, or handicapped. Methods and approaches may differ but not basic philosophy. A school's responsibility is to educate each child to become as independent as possible and take his place and function effectively in the adult world. It is desirable for visually handicapped children who can benefit from regular classroom instruction to do so. Such experiences can be a realistic preparation for living as adults in a seeing community.

Educating Visually Handicapped Students in Public Schools

Most visually handicapped students need some assistance to keep up academically with their seeing classmates. Teachers especially trained to meet needs of visually handicapped children should be, and usually are, employed to teach blind and partially seeing boys and girls. Additional expenses of transportation, Braille and large print books, Braille writers, and other such equipment, are usually supplied to school districts through state and federal governments. Thus, to give visually handicapped children an adequate education should cost most school districts no more than educating children with normal vision.

Experience has shown that with additional assistance, most visually handicapped boys and girls can be trained to earn respectable livings in adulthood. The aim is to train useful citizens, rather than individuals who will be wards of society and given pensions by the government. To aid blind students in achieving this goal, their teachers must truly believe in this basic concept.

Basically three approaches are used in public schools to educate blind and partially seeing boys and girls: (1) self-contained classes, (2) resource rooms, and (3) itinerant teachers. In the self-contained class, students receive all their formal instruction in one room. This room contains necessary special books and equipment and devices, and should be well lighted. Boys and girls are transported, usually by taxi or mini-bus, from all parts of the city to the school where this class is located. Visually handicapped students in self-contained classes usually have little contact on the campus with boys and girls of normal vision.

In the resource room approach, a visually handicapped child is assigned to a regular classroom and spends most of his time there with children who have normal vision. Transportation is provided to the site of the resource room. The special room and teacher are available to meet specific student needs. Resource teachers usually give instruction in Braille, arithmetic, typing, and the use of large print and magnifiers. Typing is essential to these children and is usually introduced in the fourth grade. Resource teachers also interpret the program to other teachers, principals, other school personnel, and parents. Often special teachers will find it necessary to prepare Braille or large type materials for students to use in their regular classrooms.

In itinerant programs, the blind or partially seeing students attend neighborhood elementary or secondary schools and receive individual assistance from a specially trained teacher on a scheduled basis. During the day, an itinerant teacher travels from school to school. Students in this program receive the same type of service and equipment as do those in the resource room. Itinerant teachers usually serve partially seeing students who only need large type books or special equipment, not individual instruction.

In recent years special teachers have been relieved of much transcribing. Many school districts have employed trained people to prepare materials in Braille and large type. In many places volunteers perform these valuable services.

Some states have special funds available to employ readers for the blind. Often readers are classmates who are familiar with the material and wish to earn money.

More and more public schools are employing specially trained instructors to teach orientation and mobility. The goals of this training are to provide students with necessary mechanical and conceptual skills to become safe and independent travelers in varied environments. Obviously, participation in an active and vigorous physical education program will do much to prepare students for mobility instruction.

Some public schools are accepting their responsibilities to teach living skills to visually impaired boys and girls. At present, however, this is usually done in summer school sessions. Instruction is given in housekeeping, cooking, care of clothing, sewing, use of tools and materials for making household repairs, physical activities and recreation. Many special methods and materials which blind people can use to aid them in their duties about the house are also introduced. Some blind individuals find certain products on the open market easier to use than some special devices. In any event, many blind wives do all their own housework and most sightless husbands take care of common household chores and repairs.

The general curriculum for the visually handicapped youngsters is not different from that for children with normal vision. Fulfilling class requirements may be done by reading Braille or large print and by listening to recordings, tapes, or cassettes. Teachers should make it possible for students to examine models and all sorts of specimens by touch. The range of vocational offerings may include instruction in homemaking, electronics, and shop courses with the use of power tools. Blind students, with the help of sighted classmates, should be expected to work in science laboratories. Visually impaired students should take an active part in school physical education, recreation, and camping programs.

The average blind student is likely to be educationally retarded a few months or even a year since it is often more difficult for him to obtain adequate concepts and experiences at the same age as his sighted classmates. There are, however, some very intelligent blind students as well as some who are mentally retarded. The latter type of student should be educated in classes for mentally retarded children and given assistance on a scheduled basis by a resource or itinerant teacher of visually handicapped students.

Ophthalmologists tell us that whenever possible, students with any degree of residual vision should be encouraged to use the visual avenue to enrich tactile learning experiences. Obviously school personnel have an obligation to provide good lighting for all students, particularly those who are visually impaired. Fluorescent fixtures are an excellent way to provide adequate lighting.

It is the responsibility of schools to contribute to the fullest possible development of the potentialities of all boys and girls, including those who happen to be visually impaired. Since educating visually handicapped children in all respects, physical and mental, is feasible, it remains only for all schools with blind or partially seeing children to organize and carry out complete programs of instruction and training.

Part II

ACTIVITIES FOR VISUALLY HANDICAPPED CHILDREN

All children are entitled to physical education programs designed to meet their special needs. Nearly all blind children need programs and activities to develop high levels of physical fitness. Impaired, disabled, and handicapped students need well-balanced, imaginative physical education programs to help them become useful, contributing members of society. A blind child can get proper training most of the time by being intelligently integrated into regular physical education classes or units. If a blind child is not getting sufficient vigorous activity during a class period, he should be assigned individual exercises for the duration of that period.

Some public schools and nearly all residential schools for the blind provide adequate physical éducation opportunities for visually handicapped students. Unfortunately, thousands of visually impaired children in public schools receive no physical education or are assigned activities which develop little in terms of physical fitness. The material on the following pages is presented to provide information to help personnel in all schools to organize adequate physical activity programs for their visually handicapped youngsters.

Chapter 6

EVALUATION AND PHYSICAL FITNESS

When a visually handicapped child enters a physical education class, the teacher needs to obtain information on his physical capabilities, including overall motor ability and physical fitness level. Information can be obtained from the resource or itinerant teacher who, if possible, should be present when the visually impaired child first enters the physical education class and, if needed, for a few days afterward. Physical education teachers can learn a great deal about a blind child's orientation ability by observing him enter the class. More can be learned by observing his reactions to various pieces of equipment. Does he know what each one is? Does he know how to use each one? Is he willing to experiment and find out? In this way a physical educator gains some general impressions of a blind student's capabilities, strengths, weaknesses, accuracy in mobility, coordination, courage, willingness to explore, receptiveness to instruction, confidence, self-image, and many other physical and personal traits.

The teacher may then wish to explore other activities with a student. He may, for example, ask a child to run a short dash, do sit-ups, push-ups, pull-ups, or a standing long jump. If swimming is part of the program, the teacher may ask a blind student to enter the shallow end of the pool and observe his reactions. A mobile boy or girl has no difficulty walking or swimming around a pool and locating the diving board; a hesitant, timid, or frightened student needs someone to show him around the pool in great detail. This discovery or exploration approach enables a teacher to learn much about each visually handicapped child. Physical educators are then in much better positions to organize activity programs to meet the needs of each visually handicapped youngster.

The facts on blindness previously discussed should be kept in mind by each instructor as he becomes acquainted with different visually handicapped students. A great deal of observation and experimentation may be required to understand what each child with some useful vision can see and what he cannot see. Partially seeing youngsters may be able to see some things under one set of light conditions and not under another. Also, children with similar eye reports often do not see things in the same way since some make much better use of their vision than others. Physical educators should encourage each child to use as much vision as possible, and be wary of the reasons some students give to be excused from certain activities. It is reassuring to know that only a small percentage of visually handicapped children have eye conditions which could be endangered by vigorous activity.

Physical Performance Evaluation

Until recently, measuring performances in such activities as pull-ups, flexed arm hang for girls, standing long jump, and the 50-yard dash was believed to be obtaining information on physical fitness. Today most of the items used on the AAHPERD Youth Fitness Test between 1955 and 1980 are now considered to be measures of performance related to athletic ability. Such activities are an important part of the physical education program. How can a physical educator obtain meaningful measurements of performances of visually impaired boys and girls?

Sightless and visually handicapped children can be expected to perform on an equal basis with their sighted peers in some activities. The regular norms and testing procedures can be used for pull-ups, arm hang, standing long jump, sit-ups, squat-thrusts, and push-ups. Special norms are needed to measure performances of partially seeing and sightless boys and girls in the 50-yard dash. Partially sighted children can run such a dash without assistance, and can complete the event in a shorter time than a sightless child. A sightless boy or girl can run 50 yards by running his fingers lightly along a sash cord, stretched out tightly between two people. Some runners may prefer to place a section of rubber hose or plastic tubing over the rope, and then slide it along the rope. This prevents skin injuries to inexperienced sightless runners. In any event, the average sightless runner does not move as fast as a partially sighted child, and an average partially sighted child does not run 50 yards as fast as an average sighted peer. For this reason, separate norms are needed to measure the performances of visually handicapped and sightless boys and girls. These norms are presented below.

ADJUSTED NORMS FOR BLIND AND PARTIALLY SEEING GIRLS

50–Yard Dash For Blind Girls

Percen-tile	10 Yr.	11 Yr.	12 Yr.	13 Yr.	14 Yr.	15 Yr.	16 Yr.	17 Yr.	Percen-tile
100	8.4	8.1	7.8	7.4	7.4	7.5	7.3	7.5	100
95	9.0	8.7	8.4	7.9	7.9	8.0	7.8	8.0	95
90	9.5	9.1	8.8	8.3	8.3	8.4	8.2	8.4	90
85	10.0	9.6	9.2	8.7	8.7	8.8	8.6	8.8	85
80	10.5	10.1	9.6	9.1	9.1	9.2	9.0	9.2	80
75	11.0	10.6	10.0	9.5	9.5	9.6	9.4	9.6	75
70	11.5	11.0	10.4	9.8	9.8	9.9	9.7	9.9	70
65	12.0	11.4	10.8	10.1	10.1	10.2	10.0	10.2	65
60	12.4	11.8	11.2	10.4	10.4	10.5	10.3	10.5	60
55	12.9	12.2	11.6	10.8	10.8	10.8	10.6	10.8	55
50	13.3	12.7	12.0	11.2	11.2	11.2	11.0	11.2	50
45	14.2	13.5	12.8	11.7	11.7	11.8	11.6	11.8	45
40	15.2	14.4	13.6	12.3	12.3	12.4	12.2	12.4	40
35	16.2	15.3	14.4	12.9	12.9	13.0	12.8	13.0	35
30	17.2	16.2	15.2	13.6	13.6	13.6	13.4	13.6	30
25	18.2	17.1	16.0	14.3	14.3	14.3	14.1	14.3	25
20	19.2	18.0	16.7	15.0	15.0	15.1	14.9	15.1	20
15	20.2	18.8	17.4	15.8	15.8	15.9	15.7	15.9	15
10	21.2	19.7	18.2	16.6	16.6	16.7	16.5	16.7	10
5	22.2	20.6	19.0	17.5	17.5	17.5	17.3	17.5	5
0	24.1	22.8	20.8	20.1	20.2	20.5	19.8	21.0	0

50–Yard Dash For Partially Seeing Girls

Percentile	10 Yr.	11 Yr.	12 Yr.	13 Yr.	14 Yr.	15 Yr.	16 Yr.	17 Yr.	Percentile
100	7.3	7.0	6.7	6.4	6.2	6.2	6.4	6.4	100
95	8.2	7.9	7.5	7.5	7.2	7.2	7.5	7.5	95
90	8.5	8.3	8.1	7.9	7.6	7.6	7.9	7.9	90
85	8.8	8.6	8.4	8.2	7.9	7.9	8.2	8.2	85
80	9.0	8.8	8.6	8.5	8.2	8.2	8.5	8.5	80
75	9.2	9.0	8.9	8.8	8.5	8.5	8.8	8.8	75
70	9.6	9.4	9.2	9.1	8.7	8.8	9.1	9.1	70
65	9.9	9.7	9.5	9.3	8.9	9.0	9.3	9.3	65
60	10.3	10.0	9.8	9.6	9.2	9.2	9.6	9.6	60
55	10.6	10.3	10.0	9.8	9.4	9.4	9.8	9.8	55
50	11.0	10.6	10.3	10.0	9.6	9.6	10.0	10.0	50
45	11.8	11.3	10.9	10.5	10.0	10.0	10.5	10.5	45
40	12.6	12.0	11.5	11.0	10.5	10.5	11.0	11.0	40
35	13.4	12.7	12.1	11.5	11.1	11.0	11.5	11.5	35
30	14.2	13.4	12.7	12.0	11.6	11.5	12.0	12.0	30
25	15.0	14.2	13.4	12.6	12.2	12.0	12.6	12.6	25
20	15.8	14.9	14.0	13.2	12.9	12.7	13.2	13.2	20
15	16.6	15.7	14.7	13.8	13.5	13.4	13.8	13.8	15
10	17.4	16.4	15.4	14.4	14.1	14.0	14.4	14.4	10
5	18.2	17.1	16.1	15.0	14.8	14.7	16.0	15.0	5
0	19.9	19.2	18.8	17.0	16.9	16.5	17.1	17.3	0

ADJUSTED NORMS FOR BLIND AND PARTIALLY SEEING BOYS

50–Yard Dash for Blind Boys

Percentile	10 Yr.	11 Yr.	12 Yr.	13 Yr.	14 Yr.	15 Yr.	16 Yr.	17 Yr.	Percentile
			Percentile Scores Based on Age						
100	8.7	8.0	7.6	7.2	6.9	6.6	6.3	6.0	100
95	9.3	8.5	8.2	7.8	7.5	7.1	6.8	6.5	95
90	9.5	8.7	8.4	8.0	7.7	7.3	7.0	6.7	90
85	9.7	8.9	8.6	8.2	7.9	7.5	7.2	6.9	85
80	9.9	9.1	8.7	8.3	8.0	7.6	7.3	7.0	80
75	10.1	9.3	8.9	8.5	8.2	7.8	7.5	7.2	75
70	10.3	9.5	9.1	8.7	8.4	8.0	7.7	7.4	70
65	10.5	9.7	9.3	8.8	8.5	8.1	7.8	7.5	65
60	10.7	9.9	9.5	9.0	8.7	8.3	8.0	7.7	60
55	10.9	10.1	9.6	9.1	8.8	8.4	8.1	7.8	55
50	11.1	10.3	9.8	9.3	9.0	8.6	8.3	8.0	50
45	11.4	10.6	10.1	9.6	9.3	8.9	8.6	8.3	45
40	11.6	10.8	10.3	9.8	9.5	9.1	8.8	8.5	40
35	11.9	11.1	10.6	10.1	9.8	9.4	9.1	8.8	35
30	12.1	11.3	10.8	10.3	10.0	9.6	9.3	9.0	30
25	12.4	11.6	11.1	10.6	10.3	9.9	9.6	9.3	25
20	12.7	11.9	11.4	10.9	10.6	10.2	9.9	9.6	20
15	13.0	12.2	11.7	11.2	10.9	10.5	10.2	9.9	15
10	13.4	12.6	12.1	11.6	11.3	10.9	10.6	10.3	10
5	13.7	12.9	12.4	11.9	11.6	11.2	10.9	10.6	5
0	21.0	19.5	18.5	17.6	16.6	15.7	14.7	13.8	0

50-Yard Dash for Partially Seeing Boys

Percen-tile	10 Yr.	11 Yr.	12 Yr.	13 Yr.	14 Yr.	15 Yr.	16 Yr.	17 Yr.	Percen-tile
100	7.3	7.0	6.7	6.4	6.2	5.9	5.6	5.4	100
95	7.8	7.6	7.3	7.0	6.7	6.4	6.1	5.9	95
90	8.0	7.7	7.5	7.2	6.9	6.6	6.4	6.1	90
85	8.2	7.9	7.7	7.4	7.1	6.8	6.5	6.2	85
80	8.3	8.0	7.8	7.5	7.2	6.9	6.6	6.3	80
75	8.4	8.1	7.9	7.6	7.3	7.0	6.7	6.4	75
70	8.5	8.2	8.0	7.7	7.4	7.1	6.8	6.5	70
65	8.6	8.3	8.1	7.9	7.6	7.2	6.9	6.6	65
60	8.8	8.5	8.3	8.0	7.7	7.4	7.1	6.8	60
55	8.9	8.6	8.4	8.2	7.9	7.5	7.2	6.9	55
50	9.2	8.8	8.7	8.5	8.1	7.6	7.3	7.0	50
45	9.5	9.1	8.9	8.6	8.3	7.9	7.6	7.3	45
40	10.0	9.4	9.1	8.8	8.5	8.2	7.9	7.5	40
35	10.4	9.8	9.5	9.1	8.8	8.5	8.2	7.8	35
30	10.7	10.1	9.8	9.4	9.1	8.7	8.4	8.0	30
25	11.0	10.4	10.1	9.7	9.4	9.0	8.7	8.3	25
20	11.4	10.8	10.5	10.1	9.7	9.3	9.0	8.6	20
15	11.8	11.2	10.9	10.5	10.1	9.7	9.3	8.9	15
10	12.3	11.7	11.3	10.9	10.5	10.0	9.7	9.3	10
5	12.7	12.1	11.7	11.3	10.9	10.4	10.0	9.6	5
0	16.6	15.1	14.7	14.3	13.3	12.4	11.9	11.4	0

Charles Buell[1] has developed achievement scales in swimming, rope jumping, rope climbing, and other events which can be used to measure the performances of partially sighted and sightless boys and girls. These achievement scales are based upon the performances of a representative sample of about 3,000 visually handicapped boys and girls. Confidence can be placed in these norms, and they can be used to measure performances of blind children in public schools or in residential schools for the blind.

By comparing a student's percentile or normative scores in various events, his strengths and weaknesses can be determined. Achievement scales can be used as motivational devices, since most students are interested in comparing present with previous performances to determine their improvement. It is also fair to use such scales to conduct competition between visually impaired children and their sighted peers. It is just as difficult for a blind child to achieve the 50th percentile on an achievement scale developed for him as it is for his sighted peer to reach the same percentile on the regular scale. A rating of each blind child's performance, progress, and development can and should become a part of his permanent record.

[1]Buell, Charles. *Physical Education for Blind Children.* 2d ed. Springfield, IL: Charles Thomas, 1982.

The Health Related Physical Fitness Test

The term physical fitness has taken on a new meaning in recent years. A clear differentiation has been made between physical fitness related primarily to functional health, and physical performance related primarily to athletic ability. AAHPERD took the lead in developing the new concept of physical fitness related to health. The following criteria were used to select items for a physical fitness test:

1. A physical fitness test should measure a range which extends from severely limited dysfunction to high levels of functional capacity.
2. A test should measure capacities which can be improved by participating in physical activity.
3. Test scores should accurately measure an individual's physical fitness.

A physical fitness test was developed to measure the amount of fat on the body, cardiorespiratory function, abdominal function, and low back hamstring musculoskeletal function. Test items include measuring the skinfold on the triceps, obtaining a time or measurement in a distance run, modified sit-ups, and sit and reach.

Such a test requires no modification for children who have enough vision to run by themselves. The regular norms can be used for them in each test. For a sightless child, the regular norms can be used in all tests except the distance run. In the distance run, a sightless child should be judged on a scale, 10 percentile points lower. If a sightless child reaches the 40th percentile, he should be given credit for having performed at the 50th percentile level. In general, the physical educator should add 10 percentile points to the actual performance of the sightless child. This will give a fair measurement of a sightless child's cardiorespiratory fitness. The reason for making the distinction is that a sightless child will normally run with a sighted runner in a manner which slows both of them. The blind runner can run beside the sighted runner and touch elbows from time to time, or hold the elbow of his sighted partner. In each case, the running is somewhat slowed.

If the instructor does grant a concession of 10 or less percentile points, he should still award the same certificates and chevrons. AAHPERD has given permission to make reasonable concessions to legally blind and sightless boys and girls.

The norms and percentile points used for scoring in the AAHPERD *Health Related Physical Fitness Test* are very useful to the teacher and the student. Research indicates that the test accurately measures fitness related to health. The percentile norms tell the teacher that the student meets average physical fitness requirements, and if not, how far below average the student is performing. The test results can be used to identify the areas in which a student needs to improve in physical fitness. The instructor can then prescribe a program of exercises to bring about the needed improvement. Also, the percentile norms can be used to motivate a pupil to improve his physical fitness. Those who need it, should be encouraged to work toward the 25th percentile. When that goal has been attained, a student is urged to work toward the 50th percentile, or average performance.

The Importance of Physical Fitness for Visually Impaired Persons

Physical fitness is important for everyone, but blind individuals have a special need for high levels of functional health. Visually impaired and sightless individuals expend more energy to reach the same goals as their sighted peers. For example, a person with little or no vision must work harder to find objects around the house or classroom. Touch is not as efficient as is vision. In dusting or cleaning a floor a blind person must work harder to be certain the job is completed satisfactorily. Walking alone along a street requires a blind person to be more alert than his sighted peers. To be alert, one must use additional energy. In almost every activity, a blind person works harder. The expectation today is that blind boys and girls will grow to be adults and take their places in the regular world of industry. This definitely requires physical fitness.

Ideas to Stimulate Fitness

In schools for the blind, many students participate in 50- and 100-mile walking or jogging clubs and receive certificates and awards when specific milestones are reached. Other students earn certificates in 10- and 50-mile swim programs sponsored by the American Red Cross. Visually handicapped students in public schools can be challenged and motivated by similar activities and approaches.

Students with visual handicaps, particularly at the high school level, should be encouraged by teachers and parents to participate in individualized aerobic programs in their spare time. Hopefully, these programs will be carried into adulthood. Swimming, stationary running, rope skipping, and exercise on a stationary trainer bicycle or treadmill need no modification for blind individuals. Some blind people walk rapidly without a cane, but they are usually safer with one. A sightless person can jog, hike, or use a tandem bicycle with a sighted partner. Persons with some useful vision can exercise by themselves. Individuals with even less than one tenth of normal vision can safely cycle in areas where there is little or no traffic. Since visually handicapped individuals need superior levels of physical fitness to succeed, they should be encouraged to become permanent participants in programs that promote vigorous physical activity.

Chapter 7

SPECIAL EQUIPMENT AND TEACHING METHODS

The number of items manufactured to aid blind persons in physical education is limited. Some of them will be mentioned in this chapter, but the instructor is asked to remember that it is not necessary to have any special equipment available to include blind children in regular physical education classes. Some generally available items are discussed here because of their particular value to blind individuals. Teaching methods used in a class where one or more members happens to be blind are not radically different. Some helpful suggestions will be given, but they will not greatly change the structure of class instruction. There is room for creative physical educators, and it is hoped that new methods will be developed.

Special Equipment

About the first special item one thinks of is an audible ball. There are two basic types, and each has its advantages and disadvantages. There are "bell" balls and there are "beeper" balls. Balls manufactured with bells in them are much cheaper than "beeper" balls. A common rubber ball with bells in it is available from the American Foundation for the Blind, 15 W. 16th St., New York, NY 10011. An all-purpose ball with bells in it is also available from Flaghouse, 18 W. 18th St., New York, NY 10114. Besides being reasonably priced, bell balls are relatively more durable than beeper balls. The disadvantage of a bell ball is that a sightless person has difficulty locating such a ball when it comes to a stop. It is practical to use bell balls for a variety of ball games.

Beeper balls have batteries in them and emit a high beeping sound when a pin is removed. The beeping sound can be heard well only when there is absolute quietness in the playing area. Since this is unlikely in public school play, the balls are of limited value there. Such balls are expensive and most of them do not withstand rough play well. It is reported that the beeper baseballs now sold by the Braille Sports Foundation, 7525 North St., Minneapolis, MN 55426 and the Blind Sports Inc., 2391 Notre Dame Rd., Costa Mesa, CA 92626, do last longer. Science for the Blind, 144 Pugh Rd., Wayne, PA 19087 and Flaghouse Inc., 18 W. 18th St., New York, NY 10011 sell beeping footballs, basketballs, soccer balls, and volleyballs. The chief advantage of a beeper ball is that it can be located in a general way when it comes to a stop. Most beeper balls have a limited number of windows through which the sound is emitted. To some extent, this arrangement does not make it possible for a sightless person to reach directly for the ball. This is because, in reaching for the sound, the person may be two or three inches from the ball, since the sound is emitted from a limited number of windows.

51

It is helpful for visually impaired children to have all balls painted in bright colors. This helps those who have some useful vision to better see the balls when they are in motion.

The American Printing House for the Blind, 1839 Frankfort Ave., Louisville, KY 40206, makes available to schools and classes for the blind AC or battery-operated audible goal locators. The locators make a buzzing sound and can be placed on basketball backboards. They have been used in various ways in gymnasiums, swimming pools, and on the playground. The American Printing House also manufactures the Staley Sports Kit which is used to demonstrate play areas and strategies in some sports.

Sightless bowlers find that using a metal guide rail helps them roll the ball straighter down the lane. There are rails three feet high and nine feet long, made of aluminum which can be quickly assembled and disassembled. The rails can be taken to any bowling lane. A good source for the rails in this country is the American Foundation for the Blind.

Residential schools for the blind and a few public schools have erected guide wires which enable sightless runners to run short distances up to 100 yards in one direction, or longer if shuttling is used. Sightless students can run their fingers lightly along the wire to receive direction. In situations where it is impractical to erect guide wires, it is possible for two sighted students to stretch a sash cord tightly, while a sightless boy or girl uses it for guidance in running short distances.

In distance running, a blind student runs with a sighted person, usually holding his partner's elbow. However, there are other methods of running with a sighted partner which have proven satisfactory. One method is to run side by side, touching elbows from time to time.

Throwing balls for distance, putting the shot, and throwing the discus are usually done in circles. For blind students it is well to provide raised circles. This can be done by curving a small pipe or a hose to outline the circle.

Blind children can take part in relays better when they can easily identify the turning point. The edge of a grass surface or a gymnasium wall can be used for a turning point. Another way to run relays indoors is to use a mat surface 5 feet wide and 20 feet long. Sightless participants can run relays well on such a surface.

When one or two members of a class happen to be blind, it is well to play tag and similar activities in a limited area where goals, fences, or walls can easily be located. Gymnasiums cleared of obstacles or outdoor tennis courts are suitable areas.

There are types of equipment which can be purchased on the open market which are particularly helpful to blind persons. Such items as treadmills, jogging machines, and jump ropes are used by many sightless individuals.

Cycling is another highly regarded physical fitness activity. Trainer bicycles or tandems are appropriate for sightless children. Small training wheels can be placed on either side of the back wheel of a bicycle to increase stability and safety, or two bicycles can be placed side by side and connected by rods. Of course, a visually impaired child should be accompanied by a rider with a good deal of vision on connected and tandem bicycles. Where there is little or no traffic, some visually handicapped cyclists can safely ride alone if obstructions are not nearby.

Multi-station apparatus for weight and resistance training is ideal for blind people. Rowing machines, wall peg boards, travelling ladders, and climbing ropes are particularly useful for a blind person. Most playground items such as jungle gyms, parallel bars, and horizontal bars are suitable for visually impaired children.

More information on special equipment can be obtained from state schools for the blind and metropolitan agencies for the blind.

Providing Information on Physical Education and Recreation

When a physical educator or recreation leader needs to provide information for visually handicapped students, there are ways this can be done. Most visually handicapped boys and girls receive support from resource or itinerant teachers. It is suggested that physical educators and recreation leaders make their needs known to these teachers. It is the responsibility of these teachers to see that such information is provided in the proper form.

There are some books in large type or Braille available on sports and athletes. Also, such books are sometimes recorded on long-playing records (talking books) or tapes.

Teen-Time is a magazine in Braille and large type which carries a column on sports for the blind. For a free subscription write to *Teen-Time*, 3558 S. Jefferson Ave., St. Louis, MO 63118. *Feeling Sports* is a newsletter in large type devoted entirely to sports for the visually impaired. For subscriptions write to *Feeling Sports*, 7525 North St., Minneapolis, MN 55426. By becoming a member, one can receive a newsletter in larger type of the United

States Association for Blind Athletes, 55 W. California Ave., Beach Haven Park, NJ.

A physical educator can have books or articles transcribed into Braille or large type or recorded on tape, if he contacts the resource or itinerant teacher of the visually handicapped student. By using Braille, large type, or tape, the physical educator can make available such information as charts, records, standings, rules of a game, etc. This is not an imposition because most school districts which enroll visually handicapped students, also employ transcribers or at least make arrangements for such services. Also, most metropolitan areas have organizations which offer free transcribing services to blind students.

Teaching Methods

A blind child depends primarily upon his tactual and auditory senses to obtain information about himself and his environment. Kinesthetic awareness gives information about the position of the body and its various parts, and about other basic motor, perceptual-motor, and perceptual concepts.

When dealing with a visually handicapped individual, the teacher should give detailed auditory instructions which are in concrete terms within the individual's realm of experience and not based on visual cues. For example, defining *sway* in terms of a tree doesn't mean much to one who has never seen a tree. A student may observe the teacher or a talented student perform skills or patterns in slow motion by placing his fingers on the performer's body. Some instructors bend and maneuver large rubber dolls into desired positions so that blind students can examine actions with their fingers. Dolls are particularly valuable to convey concepts basic to forward rolls, somersaults, flips, stunts, self-testing, and related activities since it is impossible for a blind child to observe performers completely by touch. Many lead-up and less complicated activities precede instruction in more advanced stunts, skills, and movement patterns.

Another method used in teaching blind children involves grasping the student's arms or legs and guiding him through the desired movements. An instructor mechanically manipulates the child's limbs and body so he can develop kinesthetic awareness of the skill. This procedure is especially effective when combined with the opportunity to feel another performer in action.

Vocal instruction alone is of limited value to a totally blind student. For example, in teaching wrestling, a teacher or aide must get down on the mat and show a blind youngster tactually exactly what to do; a similar approach is effective on apparatus and in a swimming pool. Blind children require individual instruction from a teacher or skilled student. Sometimes regular or additional individualized instruction is given just before a class assembles or immediately after it has been dismissed.

When a game is selected for physical education class, whether on the playground or in the classroom, some concept of the whole activity should be given to sightless youngsters beforehand; then each activity can be broken down into its component parts. Normally this procedure is used in teaching motor skills to anyone, but it is particularly helpful to, and necessary for, blind children. Each part of an activity is described verbally and demonstrated manually so blind children can grasp physically, mentally, and kinesthetically how it is done. Individual movements are then slowly put together into a total activity to complete a whole-part-whole cycle of teaching.

To keep blind children aware of their progress in learning skills and motor patterns, instructors should make frequent, honest, and sincere comments to their students. Teachers can expect blind students to learn as much as others in a class, although the methods of instruction may differ. If a student is not in physical or verbal contact with a class, he may withdraw within himself and not fully take part in the learning process.

During the process of learning a game, a blind individual should be given some verbal description of its essential characteristics by á teacher or companion. A helpful guideline is to describe what anyone would want to know at certain stages in learning the game or activity. Descriptions should be given in a matter-of-fact, not sympathetic or condescending, manner.

Teaching some sightless children to jump rope can be difficult. One practical method is to have a student stand behind the teacher and place his hands on the teacher's hips. The partners jump together in this manner for a while before a rope is introduced. At first the instructor turns the rope so the child gains a sense of rhythm; later the blind child jumps alone.

Instructing partially seeing students usually does not require as much effort on the part of teachers or aides as teaching blind youngsters. With some useful vision, students can observe demonstrations done in slow motion at close range. Sometimes these children find it helpful to have their limbs manipulated or to feel the movements of a performer's body in action. It should be noted that some children use limited vision better than others. Actually, there are few physical education or recreation programs in which partially seeing children cannot participate.

Having visually handicapped children in a class need not mean more supervision for physical educators or recreation personnel. A blind participant can be paired with a youngster who has normal vision, since sighted children in almost every class or situation are willing to help and can be taught to give only necessary assistance to visually handicapped classmates. When a blind student enters a class, it is desirable to tell his classmates something of the abilities, desires, and needs of visually handicapped individuals. As a class progresses from activity to activity, a blind student, when given the opportunity, usually demonstrates his skills and gains the respect of his classmates — he no longer stands on the sidelines; he is an integral part of the group.

Conclusion

There are many ways and means to involve visually impaired children in vigorous physical education activities in public schools and community recreation programs. Some teachers and leaders are adequately meeting the challenge—others are not.

Chapter 8

INCLUDING VISUALLY HANDICAPPED CHILDREN IN
ACTIVITY PROGRAMS

Physical education programs in which blind students participate with sighted classmates are not much different from regular programs. Even in ball games, where most modifications are necessary, the class carries on as usual while a blind player uses the required adaptations.

A number of adaptations can be used at both elementary and secondary levels, but to avoid repetition, an activity is discussed on one level only.

Teachers, particularly on the elementary level, can select games, relays, contests, stunts, self-testing activities, etc. in which a visually handicapped child can take part with little or no modification; such activities should not be less vigorous than those for sighted classmates. A teacher should not water down activities for a class because of the presence of a blind child.

It is desirable for a visually handicapped student to spend as much time as possible in regular and unmodified activities. The more an activity must be modified, the more uncomfortable a blind child and his classmates become. Therefore, adaptations should be limited to absolutely necessary minor changes. This is an important way for visually handicapped students to gain good self-images and to earn the respect of classmates. A blind child can benefit from some experiences with activities which have been modified for him, but they should not be prolonged or overdone.

Two major considerations in placing a blind child in a physical education class are his level of physical fitness, and, especially important from a youngster's point of view, his opportunity to have fun. There is no objection to assigning visually handicapped youngsters to adapted physical education classes if they are given opportunities to participate in vigorous activities every day. However, too many adapted programs do not offer vigorous activities because children with other handicapping conditions are in the same classes. In these situations blind students, who are rarely impaired beyond loss of vision, are better placed in regular classes and given vigorous exercises daily. Generally speaking, students who lack previous experience in physical education programs or possess low levels of physical fitness are best placed in adapted programs. Blind students should be placed in adapted programs if they can receive more exercise than being onlookers, scorekeepers or attendants in regular classes. Children with some useful vision are usually most appropriately placed in regular classes and given as much exercise as their classmates.

On the secondary level, blind students can select or be assigned to units of instruction rather than placed in classes for a semester or year. For example, a blind boy might participate in such units as wrestling, weight training, rebound tumbling, gymnastics, apparatus, physical fitness, and swimming. During the year he might spend time in three or four different classes in these units.

Elementary School

Some approaches to physical education on the elementary school level require little or no modification for blind students. Blind youngsters usually fit easily into movement education or exploration programs which are being used extensively and effectively in regular and special programs all over the country. Some visually handicapped children may need suggestions from time to time to help them explore space, carry out movements, or solve problems. For example, one who has never seen a cat or a rocket might find it difficult "to move like a cat" or "blast off like a rocket" at the command of his teacher.

In many Michigan schools the physical education curriculum is organized to make every child aware of his potential. No child has to try an activity or movement pattern for which he is not physically prepared. Impaired, disabled, and handicapped children fit well into programs of this type which are geared to individuals rather than groups.

Most singing games and other rhythmic activities for preschool and primary level children need little or no modification for visually handicapped children. On the intermediate level, some dances are more easily learned and performed by sightless children than other dances. Therefore, teachers can select dances requiring little or no modification when blind children are participating. If necessary, a blind student and his partner can hold hands during an entire formation or pattern. Rather than move about a great deal, a blind dancer and his partner can remain in a limited area for certain dances. A sighted partner usually can give needed assistance so that teachers and aides are free to perform their usual classroom duties.

In tumbling, teachers depend a great deal upon methods already discussed for teaching blind children. Most elementary school visually handicapped children can learn such movements and patterns as forward and backward rolls, armless sitdown and rise, frog stand, tip-up, head- and handstands, jump from knees to stand, double roll, knee-shoulder balance, and many other singles and doubles stunts and self-testing activities.

Parachute play is another activity in which blind children can easily participate. The whole class can do interesting things with a parachute — make waves, mountains, and umbrellas; pull, lift, and tug it; walk, jump, and gallop with it; play games under it; and do folk and square dances with it. Depending upon class needs and emphasis, parachute activities can be used to develop specific elements of physical fitness, basic motor patterns for games and lead-up activities, and a variety of rhythmic activities including folk and square dances.

Such fitness tests and activities should be a part of every elementary school program.

Blind children can compete in many races, such as the Chinaman's race, trio or quartet race, rail-riding race, wheelbarrow race, sack race, crab race, crawling race, lame dog race, and three-legged race. Many activities and movements in these races can serve as bases for relays. Sightless children adapt well to relays in which teammates work together. Examples of such partner relays are: sedan relay, Siamese twin relay, caterpillar relay, centipede relay, and donkey relay. Visually handicapped children respond to, and perform well in, relays such as dirty sock relay, leapfrog relay, military relay, pass through hoop relay, and stride relay.

Contests and competitive activities are popular with elementary school children. Games like Simon Says and stunt elimination (where first youngster performs stunt, second does this stunt plus another, etc.) need no modification for visually impaired youngsters. The weather vane game gives sightless children opportunities to develop orientation skills in ways that are fun. In a stalking contest a leader sings, blows a whistle, or makes other noises. When the leader stops making noise, he turns around to see if any player is moving.

Activities in which players depend upon verbal cues are usually fair to blind children. For example, a teacher may combine numbers, colors, and shapes with different body positions so that one, red, or square means stand; two, blue, or circle means sit; three, green, or triangle means be on the stomach; and four, yellow, or rectangle means lie on the back. When a number, color, or shape is called, the last player to take the correct position is eliminated or given another task to perform; sometimes the first player taking the correct position is permitted to rest so the less skilled and weaker youngsters get constant activity.

Most hula-hoop activities need no modification for blind youngsters. It is not uncommon to see blind students join in hula-hoop fun with sighted classmates; the same can be said for pogo sticks, stilts, skates, and related activities.

Another way for everyone to obtain beneficial exercise is to take a brisk hike. Have all the children, including blind youngsters, form pairs — for safety, companionship, social development, and fun on hikes. Blind children can also be integrated into games in which one or more players are blindfolded. For example, blind man's bluff can be played by blind and sighted children; sighted children may be asked to shout and clap hands to aid the "blind man."

Games played by couples or partners, such as partner tag and Ocean Is Stormy, are easily adapted for visually impaired and sighted youngsters. Such games and activities make it easy to include visually handicapped children without reducing enjoyment or exercise for the rest of a class.

Games which use a chain formation are ideal for blind children. In chain tag, for example, It catches another player; these two join hands and run to catch a third youngster, and so on until all but one is caught. The last one becomes It for the following game or chooses the next activity. A blind child can avoid the chain by running away from the sounds of footsteps.

Blind students can best play games such as Midnight on well-defined surfaces and in limited areas — a plot of grass or dirt surrounded by a sidewalk makes a good play area. In Midnight, "chickens" run from the "blind fox." On a grass surface, they should clap hands or shout;

on concrete, the "blind fox" runs toward the sound of footsteps to tag someone. When a blind youngster is a "chicken" he can run to the edge of the surface or run with a sighted partner.

Kickball is a popular game played by elementary school children. An audible ball or a regular ball rigged for sound makes a blind child's play possible and meaningful. A blind youngster often pitches, but when the ball is returned to him it should be rolled, not thrown. A catcher can give a blind pitcher directions for delivering the ball by clapping his hands, talking, or using some other audible signal.

When a blind fielder picks up a moving ball which has been kicked, the kicker should be called out. A sightless batter may place the ball on home plate, kick it, and run to first base where a teammate is shouting. If a kick is good for more than a single base, a teammate can grasp the hand of the blind player and run with him as far as possible without being put out.

Many blind children like to play softball, but usually do not perform as well as in kickball. The ball can be placed on a batting tee so a sightless batter can hit it. Bases are run and outs are made as in kickball. A mobile blind boy can be encouraged to play deep in the outfield where he can make spectacular putouts if his teammates do not pick up rolling balls in his part of the field!

When a visually handicapped student plays dodgeball, he can be paired with a sighted classmate who helps him dodge the ball. Assistance can also be given by calling directions — north, south, east, or west — to indicate where the ball is on the circle; blind youngsters can then avoid the area called. When it is a sightless player's turn to throw the ball at someone, other players clap their hands or shout.

In volleyball a blind player may make all the serves for his team. The disadvantage, however, is that other players do not have an opportunity to serve. Although many visually impaired volleyball players throw rather than hit the ball, those who can serve by hitting the ball should do so. Another popular variation is one-bounce volleyball — identical in every respect to the regulation game except that the ball is played on the first bounce — it's fun and provides equal competition for all.

Secondary School

Flag football is a popular game in which visually handicapped students can participate. Players with little or no vision usually play center or guard line positions. The player carrying the ball shouts so sightless players can locate him and attempt a tackle. An inexpensive plastic football containing bells, and rags looped around the players' belts or waist bands help blind youngsters. Some partially seeing players have played 6- and 11-man football well enough to be selected to high school all-star teams. Each year a few partially seeing players participate in college football. An outstanding offensive tight-end, Fred Arbanis, played with the Kansas City Chiefs although blind in one eye.

Partially seeing boys and girls can compete in most regular track and field events. Certain schools for the blind send students with some useful vision to compete in track and field meets with public secondary schools. Most of these visually impaired athletes only find running hurdles, competing in the pole vault, and doing the running high jump, difficult. However, some visually impaired athletes even compete in these events.

Totally blind and low vision runners may now compete in high school distance running. The *Track and Field Rule Book* states that a runner cannot be aided, but there is one exception to this rule. "The meet director or games committee may allow visually handicapped athletes to make physical contact with a team-mate for the purpose of giving direction only, provided they do not impede or interfere with any other competitor."

Although putting the shot does not require functional vision, most sightless boys and girls who have done well in this event have had vision at some time in their lives. A few well-oriented blind boys have thrown the discus. However, this sport should be attempted under carefully supervised conditions so that there is no danger to people nearby. No modifications are needed for sightless students in the standing long and high jumps. By using methods previously described, blind boys and girls can run races of all lengths, including the marathon. A number of blind runners have completed the Boston Marathon, some in less than 3 hours. Many partially seeing, and a few sightless athletes, have won letters in high school track and field; some have gone on to win letters in college competition.

Partially seeing players adapt well to basketball, but major adaptations must be made for sightless players. Usually sightless students restrict themselves to shooting baskets and such games as Around the World. A sightless student might take all the free throws awarded to sighted players. Between free throws a sightless student can jump rope or participate in other physical fitness exercises on the sidelines. Admittedly, sightless children probably should not spend much time in basketball in the public schools.

Wrestling is the sport in which blind and partially seeing athletes have most distinguished themselves. Each year over six hundred impaired boys compete on interscholastic and intercollegiate wrestling teams. About twenty-five sightless and partially sighted athletes annually place in the top six sports in wrestling meets in various states. Wrestling championships have been won in the states of Alabama, Kentucky, Michigan, New Mexico, Tennessee, Texas, and Virginia by schools for the blind. A state championship has not been won in any other sport by a team of blind boys. Some colleges and universities have awarded athletic scholarships to blind wrestlers.

In high school wrestling, blind boys now compete on an equal basis with those who have normal vision. The former disadvantage of starting on the feet has been corrected by the *High School Wrestling Rule Book*. "In matches involving a sight handicapped wrestler, the finger touch method shall be used in the neutral position and initial contact shall be made from the front." Interpretations of this rule indicate that contact must be maintained until a break for a takedown is made. Initial movement on the break must be forward. This slight modification does not interfere with the sighted boy's wrestling style.

Some blind and partially seeing boys have earned various belt degrees in judo. Older girls in some schools for the blind are given instruction in judo so they can protect themselves.

Individual competitions in which contact is maintained — for example the Indian wrestle, back to back lift, back to back push, back to back stick pull, hoop tug, boundary tug, medicine ball wrestle, hand wrestle, lifting contest, pull over, and stick pull — are fair to visually handicapped children. Games such as tug-of-war and push ball should not be overlooked since sightless youngsters can participate and the rest of the class often enjoys such changes of pace.

Swimming is only slightly more difficult to teach to blind students than to youngsters with normal vision. A blind child needs to maintain close contact with his teacher during the learning process; by swimming beside a wall of the pool, a blind swimmer can keep his direction better. Competitive swimming is possible but difficult for sightless persons. For example, in back stroke races someone must warn blind youngsters when they are approaching the wall so they will not strike their heads. Partially seeing swimmers face few problems in competitive swimming, although some may have difficulty keeping track of the opposition. Synchronized swimming is an excellent activity for visually handicapped girls.

It is common practice for partially seeing and sightless persons to dive from three-foot boards, and some also use high boards. Teaching a blind child to dive is similar to instructing him in tumbling. For the safety of the diver and other people in the pool, a visually handicapped diver should not leave the board until an all-clear signal is heard.

Blind students should be included in surfing and scuba diving instruction. They should also be included in life saving training — at least one blind father has rescued his child from the bottom of a family pool!

Some high schools and many universities have rowing crews. From time to time blind and partially seeing young men have won letters in rowing. About the only aid needed is an ordinary thumbtack pushed into an oar so a blind boy can rotate the oar to the proper position for feathering.

Gymnastic activities have long been a part of physical education programs for blind youngsters in residential schools. Blind and partially seeing boys have won letters in high school and college gymnastics — particularly in rope climbing events. Partially seeing boys and girls can take part meaningfully, in sports such as soccer, speedball, and field hockey. These sports, however, are not recommended for sightless children.

Blind and partially seeing boys and girls can take part in trampolining. A bell attached underneath the center of the trampoline helps a sightless student stay in the proper position as he performs individual stunts and routines. With proper precautions, blind children can be taught various drops and flips safely. Only a few sightless students can be safely taught more complicated stunts.

Weight training needs no modification for sightless boys. It is surprising that more do not take part in this activity.

Unfortunately bowling is not a part of the physical education program in many schools. Since this activity has much carry-over value, particularly for visually impaired students, a special effort should be made to offer bowling instruction. Many sightless bowlers use guide rails; some maintain their orientation to the alley and pins by using the wall close to an end lane.

Some visually handicapped girls twirl batons well enough to take part in parades. It usually takes them somewhat longer to learn this skill but many have developed interesting routines.

Partially seeing and even some sightless girls have been members of drill teams. For example, visually handicapped girls form one third of the drill team from the West Virginia School for the Deaf and Blind which is invited to appear in most big parades in that state.

Partially seeing students participate in dual sports such as badminton, handball, tennis, table tennis, horseshoes, and tetherball. Sightless persons can learn to play shuffleboard, and sometimes golf, but usually need quite a bit of assistance from a sighted companion.

Not many schools include winter sports in their programs. Little or no modifications are required for sightless boys and girls in sledding and tobogganing. A sightless skier usually goes down a slope behind a partner who plays a radio or makes a continuous noise of some kind. Ice skating and saucer sliding are enjoyed in pairs, however, at least one partner should have some useful vision.

Some blind secondary school students may have an opportunity to fence. Fencing equipment which is entirely safe to use without protective equipment is now available. Some teachers feel fencing makes definite contributions to the sensory development of visually handicapped children.

It is becoming increasingly important to provide children with opportunities to develop lifetime sport skills. Skill development is as important for blind children as for those with normal vision. Activities in which blind adults are most likely to participate are swimming, diving, scuba diving, water skiing, surfing, pedal boating, hiking, bowling, weight training, calisthenics, rope jumping, tandem cycling, trainer bike exercising, rowing machine exercising, winter sports, shuffle board, camping, horseback riding, and fishing.

Chapter 9

NATIONAL SPORTS ORGANIZATIONS FOR THE BLIND

Today there are a number of organizations offering sports and recreation programs to blind people on a national basis. Since this publication is devoted to mainstreaming, some explanation should be made for including such organizations.

Most of the national organizations offer more or less segregated programs of sports and recreation to blind individuals. For the most part, groups of blind people are brought together to participate or compete with one another. Of course, there are sighted people who serve as teachers, guides, helpers, etc. However, this is not mainstreaming in the true sense of the word. The United States Association for Blind Athletes offers one sport, the 10k run, in which blind and sighted athletes compete. Also, this organization distributes printed information on mainstreaming. It is possible to increase mainstreaming activities in a number of these organizations.

There are sports in which blind people cannot compete with sighted peers on an equal basis. Sightless baseball players require modifications to enjoy the game. An organization like the National Beep Baseball Association makes it possible for sightless players to win championships in baseball. Seldom does a sightless runner compete on an equal basis with his sighted peers in the 60 yd. or 60m dash. However, the United States Association for Blind Athletes makes it possible for a sightless sprinter to win national and international championships in his event. So, these organizations have added new dimensions to the lives of many blind people.

Sports organizations for the blind offer important services. They offer blind people the opportunity to develop skills. At some point, most of them can and should enter the mainstream and participate and compete with their sighted peers. For some individuals the period of development will take longer than for others. There are some who do not need extra training, and can directly enter into the mainstream. For example, there are visually impaired athletes on interscholastic and intercollegiate athletic teams.

One group who can benefit a great deal from such programs are those who have recently lost their vision. Usually these people need help to adjust to the loss of some or all of their sight. They need to learn new ways to participate and compete in sports and recreation. Sports organizations for the blind can help.

Here are brief descriptions of some of the programs which are being offered on a national basis. In addition, addresses of other organizations will be mentioned. Also, one should explore to see if any agency for the blind exists in his community.

American Blind Bowling Association

The oldest national organization offering a sports service to blind people is the American Blind Bowling Association, 150 N. Bellaire Ave., Louisville, KY 40206 (502) 896–8030. The ABBA has been sanctioning blind bowling leagues and tournaments for years. The Association also makes awards of medals and chevrons for high games, triplicate games, and split conversions. ABBA sponsors an annual national tournament which today draws more than 2,000 bowlers. The annual membership fee is $3.00.

Blind Outdoor Leisure Development (BOLD)

For much of his life, Jean Eymere enjoyed all outdoor sports as a man with normal vision. Then he lost his vision and went through several weeks of hopelessness. One day he discovered he could ski with a sighted friend. He further discovered he could climb mountains, fish, and swim without sight. It occurred to him to share this knowledge with other sightless individuals. In 1970, the Blind Outdoor Leisure Development program was founded. Each week a group of blind people come to Aspen, Colorado to receive instruction in outdoor sports. The program continues to grow and many local chapters have been formed. The BOLD program has been widely publicized in newspaper and television stories. Two motion pictures are available from BOLD, 533 E. Main St., Aspen, CO 81611 (303) 925–8922.

HEALTHsports, Inc., and the Vinland National Center

Since its beginning in 1964, the Knights Race in Norway has grown to the point where hundreds of blind skiers and their sighted guides ski cross-country after a week's training. In 1975, the same concept became a reality in the United States as the Ski for Light Race. Under the sponsorship of the Sons of Norway, Ski for Light grew rapidly and expanded in 1979 to become HEALTHsports, Inc., 1455 W. Lake St., Minneapolis, MN 55408 (612) 827–3232. Although skiing is an important sport, the organization has developed programs in other outdoor sports. Besides an International Ski for Light Race each year, there are regional races in various parts of the United States. Sport for Health is a week-long program of daily training in such activities as tandem biking, swimming, canoeing, ball games with audible balls, hiking, and training for fitness. Each visually impaired person has a sighted guide. Participation, rather than competition, is emphasized. It is hoped that after a week's training in sports, the blind individual will return home and continue participation in sports with family and friends. There are no paid personnel. Guides and other volunteers pay their own expenses. Actually, many thousands of sighted people around the United States have volunteered their services and traveled to the site for training at their own expense. To date, more than 8,000 blind and mobility handicapped persons have participated. Disabled participants and their able-bodied guides equally benefit from the activities.

HEALTHsports, Inc. acts as a resource and volunteer group as well as a delivery system for health promotion and fitness-oriented ideals and goals. A sports center for blind and other individuals is being financed in part by fund-raising and contributions. The president of HEALTHsports is a blind man, Bud Keith. The center is the Vinland National Center, 3675 Induhapi Rd., Loretto, MN 55357 (612) 479–3555. The Vinland National Center is located on a 175-acre piece of land, 23 miles west of Minneapolis. There is a 2000 foot sandy beach on Independence Lake and open and wooded spaces which are ideal for outdoor sports. An auditorium for conferences, an education building, a gymnasium, a swimming pool, hiking and riding trails, horse stables, etc. are in the process of being built.

Vinland was started with a gift of $200,000 from Norway to the American people in 1976. This was later matched by $200,000 from the Minnesota legislature. In 1978 a planning grant in the amount of $600,000 was appropriated by the U.S. Congress. In 1982, Vinland received grants from the U.S. Rehabilitation Service. HEALTHsports, Inc. and Vinland are based on the experience of the Beitostolen Health Sports Center in Norway.

National Beep Baseball Association

Beep baseball has been growing in recent years. A few years ago the National Beep Baseball Association, 512 - 8th Ave. N.E., Minneapolis, MN 55413 was organized. Today there are 32 teams and 500 members in the association. Beep baseball is played with an electronic ball which makes a beeping sound. The rules of the game may be obtained from the address listed above.

Special Olympics

Special Olympics, 1701 K St. N.W., Suite 203, Washington, DC 20006 (202) 331–1346 includes some visually impaired individuals in its program.

The United States Association for Blind Athletes

In 1976, the U.S. participated in the first Olympics for the Blind which was held in Canada. This sparked the formation of a permanent organization to sponsor regional, national, and international competition for blind athletes of both sexes in track and field, swimming, wrestling, gymnastics, powerlifting, Nordic and Alpine skiing, and goal ball. The latter game is played by rolling an audible ball past the opposing team and over the goalline. The United States Association for Blind Athletes (USABA) was formed in 1976, with a head office at 55 W. California Ave., Beach Haven Park, NJ 08008 (609) 492–1017. Membership can be obtained by sending $7.00 to the main office. USABA publishes a newsletter, covering the national and international scenes in sports for the blind. When funds permit, the organization distributes, free of charge, printed materials on mainstreaming.

An 800m race in the 1980 Olympics for the Blind, Holland.

Each year the USABA holds national championships for hundreds of blind athletes from over 30 states. In 1978, USABA hosted the first North American Games for the Blind. Teams of blind athletes have been sent abroad to compete, in some cases to interest other countries in international competition for blind athletes.

In 1980 the second Olympics for the Blind was held in Holland. USABA sent 50 athletes who won more medals than did any other country. USABA is scheduled to host the 1984 Olympics for the Blind in our country. This organization is affiliated with the International Blind Sports Association (IBSA), which was organized in 1981.

The U.S. Olympic Committee (USOC) made a grant of $50,000 to USABA in 1982. The organization has been benefitting also from smaller grants from various foundations.

International competition brings the same experiences to blind athletes as it does to those who have normal vision. One experiences a great deal of pride in representing his country. Our blind athletes have gained many of the other values commonly found in international competition and foreign travel.

USABA has chartered chapters in fifteen states, and there are organizations in another fifteen states which are working toward affiliation with the organization. The local chapters have raised the funds needed to send the blind athletes on trips abroad. The affiliates have also organized local programs in various sports.

From the beginning, a blind man, Arthur Copeland, has been president of USABA. Other than some part-time secretarial service, USABA has no paid personnel.

The United States Blind Golfers Association

Each year the United States Blind Golfers Association, 6026 Menjamin St., New Orleans, LA 70118 (504) 891–4737 holds a national tournament, which is limited to 25 sightless players. These tournaments have been held for about 30 years with the winners posting scores of about 200 for 36 holes. The sightless golfer's club is placed behind the ball by his sighted coach. The club is then drawn backward by the sightless golfer, and he then makes his swing. The number of sightless golfers is quite limited.

Other Organizations Offering Sports Programs to Blind People

American Blind Skiing Foundation
34 S. Main
Mount Prospect, IL 60056

American Camping Association
Bradford Woods
Martinsville, IN 46151

Colorado Outdoor Education Center for the Handicapped
P.O. Box 697
Breckenridge, CO 80424

Handicapped Boaters Association
P.O. Box 1134 Ansonia Station
New York, NY 10023

National Handicapped Sports and Recreation Association
P.O. Box 18664 Capitol Hill Station
Denver, CO 80218

National Inconvenienced Sportsmen's Association
3738 Walnut Ave.
Carmichael, CA 95608

U.S. Braille Chess Association
c/o Mac Garnor
Rt. #5
Maryville, TN 37801

Chapter 10

RECREATION AND VISUALLY HANDICAPPED CHILDREN

Most leisure-time activities are feasible for visually impaired persons although slight modifications are sometimes necessary and desirable. Some blind and partially sighted children may need adaptations and special techniques since they use touch instead of vision. Many visually handicapped children do not participate in a wide range of community recreational activities because of the attitudes of people about them, not because of their partial or total loss of vision. Since this problem has been discussed, it remains only to point out that the attitudes of visually handicapped children and their families are basic factors in determining success or failure in recreational activities.

A blind child's participation in recreational programs is largely determined by the adjustment he and his family make to the condition. Professional workers recognize the right of a child and his family to decide the activities, if any, in which he will participate. Certainly recreation personnel should offer guidance and encouragement but final decisions should be made by the child and his family.

Participation in recreational activities is just as important, if not more so, for blind or partially seeing children as for their peers with normal vision. These programs and their objectives are essentially the same for impaired, disabled, and handicapped children as for non-afflicted youngsters. The sense of confidence gained from skills developed during participation in recreational activities as a child enables individuals with handicapping conditions to live happier, more useful lives as adults. If children with handicapping conditions are to have well-developed personalities, they must work and play with physically normal individuals; they must have friends and feel there is a place for them.

Families, teachers, and recreation personnel assist visually impaired children to become useful, happy members of the community by putting into practice common sense approaches. Social experiences cannot be satisfactory when one individual pities, patronizes, or lacks respect for another. To be successful, the approach must be objective, not emotional. Visually handicapped children should be treated as human beings of worth, dignity, and ability — not as blind boys and girls.

Since visually handicapped children live in a world geared to sighted people, they should be integrated into recreational programs of public schools as well as those sponsored by community organizations and clubs. In these programs youngsters gain much more by participating than by being spectators. It is so easy to assign the latter role to a visually impaired child.

A number of activities are mentioned in this chapter as suitable for visually handicapped children; such a list is far from all-inclusive. Not

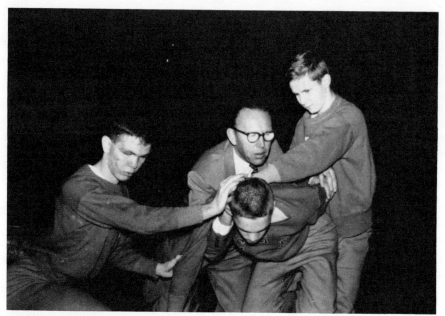

The author is shown giving wrestling instruction to three outstanding wrestlers at the California School for the Blind, Berkeley.

all blind or partially sighted children enjoy or benefit from all of these activities. Music is considered by some specialists as an ideal activity for sightless individuals. Some visually handicapped children have talent in and enjoy music while others care little for it. Since people with handicapping conditions differ from each other as do other human beings, activities must be based on the likes and dislikes of the participants rather than on preconceived notions of what others think blind people ought to enjoy. Individual differences must be recognized and emphasis placed on ability rather than disability.

Adjustment to an impairment depends primarily upon an individual's innate makeup and the effect of the environment upon his personality. If a blind child does not perform adequately in various activities, it is useless to try to bring him up to normal by indiscriminately inducing him to fill idle time with more and more participation. An individual may be enticed into many activities and still remain unhappy and poorly adjusted. Participation in more recreational activities is not the answer; the key is appropriate action conducted under conditions that stimulate growth in social adjustment and emotional stability.

Recreational Activities of Agencies for Blind Children

In many large metropolitan areas of the United States certain agencies for blind persons offer children varied recreational programs. However, in most of these programs blind children participate together, separated and segregated from children with normal vision. While such programs may fill certain needs of children who lack the background, experience, motivation, or ability to participate successfully in community recreational programs, a major goal of these agencies should be to develop each blind child to the point where he can leave the special program and participate in community programs. Agency personnel need to help families of visually impaired youngsters develop methods of constructively utilizing community resources.

Encouragement and understanding are qualities that agency workers must constantly keep in mind. If a family feels an agency is not committed to the above goals — helping the child become as independent as possible — it should consider withdrawing the child from the program. Some children benefit from separate agency programs while others do not.

Braille Trails

Park officials in a number of states and localities have placed along nature trails pedestals with affixed Braille metal plaques describing trees, bushes, leaves, etc. Usually a rope is strung from post to post alongside the trail so a blind person can guide himself. Such a specially constructed trail tends to perpetuate the stereotype of the helpless blind person.

It is much more to the point to construct a trail which all nature lovers, including those who are blind, can use together. Instead of Braille plaques, a trail should be outfitted with tape-recorded cassette or reel playbacks describing specimens. Such a trail need not have guiding devices for blind persons. A blind person can pair-up with a sighted companion as he would on any hike in the mountains. This is also the position of the American Foundation for the Blind.

Role of Parent or Recreation Personnel

Not all blind children are eager to discover and participate in new activities. A child who has been relatively inactive may be afraid that an activity is too dangerous or difficult to learn, or he may fear the reactions of sighted children to him or he may have doubts about his ability to keep up. Such a child needs a great deal of understanding, encouragement, and support from professional workers, friends, and family. Frank discussions of all fears and doubts should be carried on as long as they appear helpful. It may be desirable to give individual instruction and let a child practice certain skills that will be needed in an activity. For example, a blind child whose ice or roller skating skills are below those of sighted children in a skating group he wishes to join, can be given special or pre-instruction and encouraged to seek additional practice. Obviously a child should not be permitted to join an integrated activity until he can participate safely, successfully, and with personal satisfaction. Adults need to help each child develop his skills and overcome negative feelings about trying and taking part in recreational activities. Once this has been accomplished, a blind child can select activities which he enjoys and which strengthen his capacity to live life to its fullest.

The best friend a visually handicapped child can have is one who has an open mind and is enthusiastic about helping him succeed in community recreational activities. Such a friend seeks information from various sources such as scouting organizations, boys' and girls' groups, agencies for blind persons, and private and public associations. He makes arrangements for a visually impaired child to enter groups of the youngster's choice. If a group has never had a blind member and is reluctant to let one join, it is up to the parent or recreation specialist to convince the members. He should be specific in how a blind person can participate in the group's activities. For example, if it is a card club, he can point out that blind persons use Braille playing cards. For a group of bowlers, he can mention the guide rails used by many sightless bowlers. Templates used to pound out designs on leather or metal can be mentioned to a craft group. To help sighted members of a group feel at ease with a blind person, one can outline and discuss points of courtesy.

Recreation specialists and parents should not get bogged down in medical or psychological evaluations of visually handicapped participants. It is better to let an individual show what he can do rather than work from previously set limitations which are usually based on false preconceptions. One should make use of some consultation but not let it overshadow and dictate the child's entire program.

Each impaired, handicapped, or disabled child should be encouraged to do as much as possible for himself. Successfully completing practical tasks brings confidence to any child, particularly one with a handicapping condition. Too often these children have learned to receive much more than they have been taught to give.

Neighborhood Activities

Neighborhood recreational activities may be divided into those which are commercial, civic, organizational, and of low organization. There is a place for visually impaired children in each of these types of activities.

Commercial Activities. Blind children enjoy attending sporting events and motion pictures. If a sporting event is broadcast, a blind child can take along a transistor radio and listen; otherwise a sighted companion can give a running commentary. Band music, crowd reactions, hot dogs, soft drinks, and the thrill of being present at an exciting contest mean much to anyone. At a motion picture some scenes require a brief description from a companion. Some films are more suitable for blind viewers than others since dialogue is preferred to cartoons and slapstick comedy.

Concerts and the theater present no problems for visually impaired persons. Most concessions at carnivals, fairs, and playlands can be fully enjoyed by blind youngsters depending, of course, on their age and readiness for specific activities.

Civic Activities. Civic offerings in a neighborhood usually include activities in parks, museums, zoos, etc. A sighted companion can give descriptions at a zoo or museum; sometimes those in charge permit blind children to touch animals or specimens. Some places have keys for sale that turn on descriptive records. Boating, skating, swimming, bowling, horseback riding, surfing, cycling, pedal boating, water skiing, and other physical activities have been described.

Organization Activities. Most organizations found in a neighborhood have much to offer blind children. Many visually impaired youngsters participate in dramatics, crafts, dancing, and other physical and recreational activities at YMCAs-YWCAs, Boys Clubs, and Future Farmers of America programs. Many more children need to take advantage of opportunities and participate in these programs. Cub Scouts, Boy Scouts, Girl Scouts, and Campfire Girls have handbooks available in Braille and large print. These organizations have recently revised badge requirements by including more options so that modifications are no longer necessary for visually handicapped boys and girls. The Boy Scouts have prepared a booklet entitled *Scouting For the Visually Handicapped*, and the Girl Scouts have *Handicapped Girls Girl Scouting: A Guide For Leaders.* The Scouts are eager to serve blind and partially seeing boys and girls. A parent or adult friend of a blind child can do a service for his community and the child by sponsoring a club or becoming a committee member of a scouting group.

Most neighborhoods have interest groups, primarily for teen-agers. Formal and informal clubs in amateur radio, science, chess, homemaking, and other interests have much to offer members, including those who are visually impaired. Recreational groups in churches have long been receptive to blind and partially seeing members. In these groups an impaired, disabled, or handicapped individual usually becomes acquainted quickly and soon feels he really belongs to the group.

Low Organization Activities. In low organizational activities, an understanding parent is most helpful in paving the way. A mother of a blind child can invite neighborhood children to her home for various activities. As time goes on the blind child will be invited to others' homes. At these gatherings a visually handicapped child who has a pleasing personality or a musical or athletic skill will be particularly welcome.

For games suitable for blind and sighted children, Buell's *Recreation For the Blind* is helpful. However, any game book and many elementary or secondary school physical education tests or special activity publications contain games and related activities suitable for visually impaired players.

A wise parent can find many ways to involve his visually impaired child in neighborhood activities without interfering with the interests of others. Understanding the effects of blindness and having complete confidence in the child's abilities are keys to such an approach. Usually a parent and his child must take the initiative and not expect neighbors to come to them. Consultation with personnel experienced in working with visually impaired children is helpful.

Family Activities

A blind person has enough problems without having his development interfered with by emotional or uninformed parents. A child can attain normal social development by playing and working with others, not by being alone. Some parents let their visually handicapped children listen to radio, television, tapes, and records hour after hour while other members of the family participate in a variety of recreational activities. A blind child who is denied play opportunities often retreats into fantasy; he learns little about the world, what is real and what is not. His needs for exercise and companionship are denied him. If this practice is continued for years during childhood, it is extremely difficult, if not impossible, for such an individual to have and maintain normal social relationships as an adult. Parents of blind children want their offspring to grow into useful and happy adults. It is unfortunate that some parents do not have sufficient knowledge or emotional maturity to assume their responsibilities because help is available and should be sought.

A blind child needs to be included in family activities just as much as his siblings. Some mothers, for example, leave their blind children in an automobile while they shop. Think what a blind child can learn by touch in a grocery, hardware, or variety store.

Table games are possible for blind youngsters but often need some modifications. Braille playing cards and dominoes with raised spots are used. Checkers and chess are played on boards with raised squares; checkers are round and square, while chess figures are identified by pins on top to differentiate between the two sides. These and other table games can be purchased from the American Foundation for the Blind, New York City.

Every family should camp together; blind children enjoy this greatly. They also look forward to trips to snowy areas for winter sports. Fishing is just as popular with blind individuals as for anyone else. The companionship and exhilarating feeling of being in the open and other features of hiking appeal to all boys and girls, including those with visual impairments.

Don't discard sightseeing and tours. An individual does not need vision to be thrilled by standing on a spot where history was made.

Most children yearn to do simple cooking; a wise mother includes her visually impaired child in this activity. Blind boys and girls should be encouraged to care for a pet or plant a simple garden. Other activities commonly engaged in by visually impaired children include leathercraft, weaving, ceramics, woodwork, and needlecraft.

In view of the availability of such a wide variety of recreational and leisure-time activities, there is no logical reason for visually impaired persons to miss the normal pleasures and physical, mental, and social stimulation gained from active participation in these activities.

Part III

SELECTED ANNOTATED BIBLIOGRAPHY

The first section of this bibliography lists publications and films which specifically deal with physical education and recreation for visually impaired persons. The references in the second section have been selected for their value in helping to understand the education and problems of blind persons. Most of the references in the first section are annotated, while those in the second section are not.

Books and Pamphlets

Allen, Anne. *Physical Education and Recreation for Impaired, Disabled, and Handicapped Persons: Past, Present and Future.* 1975.
   Each of the more than 20 "state of the art" reports includes a review of literature, summary of priority needs and media needs, research and demonstration, and personnel preparation. There are 17 pages devoted to the visually handicapped.
Allen, Anne. *Sports for the Handicapped.* New York: Walker and Co., 1981.
   Presents information obtained from interviews with outstanding handicapped athletes including three blind athletes.
American Foundation for the Blind. *Integrating Blind and Visually Handicapped Youths into Community Social and Recreational Programs.*
   The "how-to-do-it" pamphlet is free of charge.
American Printing House for the Blind. *Suggested Activities for the Development of Sound Localization Skills.*
   The 18-page pamphlet gives ideas for using the goal locator.
Arnheim, D.; Auxter, D.; and Crowe, W. *Principles and Methods of Adapted Physical Education.* St. Louis, MO: C. V. Mosby, 1977.
Buell, Charles. *Motor Performance of Visually Handicapped Children.* Ann Arbor, MI: Edwards Brothers, 1950. (Out of print. Summary available from author.)
Buell, Charles. *Recreation for the Blind.* New York: American Foundation for the Blind, 1951. (Out of print. Summary available from author.)
Case, Maurice. *Recreation for Blind Adults.* Springfield, IL: Charles C. Thomas, 1966.
   Many adult activities can be used for youth groups.
Chalkey, Thomas. *Your Eyes: a Book for Paramedical Personnel and the Lay Read.* Springfield, IL: Charles C. Thomas, 1974.
   The book makes eye conditions more easily understood.
Chapman, A., and Cramer, M. *Dance and the Blind Child.* New York: American Dance Guild, 1973.
Cordellos, Harry. *Breaking Through.* Mountain View, CA: Anderson World, 1981.
   An autobiography of a nationally known blind athlete.

Cratty, B. J. *Movement and Spatial Awareness in Blind Children and Youth.* Springfield, IL: Charles C. Thomas, 1971.
  Research evidence and observations are presented.
Daniels, A. S., and Davies, E. *Adapted Physical Education.* New York: Harper and Row, 1975.
  A section of the book is devoted to physical education for the blind.
Fait, Hollis. *Special Physical Education: Adapted, Corrective, Developmental.* Philadelphia: W. B. Saunders.
  One chapter is devoted to blind children.
Geddes, Delores. *Physical Activities for Individuals with Handicapping Conditions.* St. Louis, MO: C. V. Mosby, 1978.
  Practical guidelines are provided for teachers.
Hiring the Handicapped in Recreation. Washington, DC: President's Committee on Employment of the Handicapped.
Hutchison, P., and Lord, J. *Recreation Integration.* Ottawa: Leisurability Publications, 1979.
Kelley, J.D., ed. *Recreation Programming for Visually Impaired Children and Youth.* American Foundation for the Blind. 1981.
  A book recommended for recreation leaders and parents.
Kratz, Laura. *Movement without Sight.* Palo Alto, CA: Peek Publications, 1973.
  A good reference for physical educators of the blind.
Kraus, Richard. *Therapeutic Recreation Service: Principles and Practice.* Philadelphia: W. B. Saunders, 1978.
  The book contains more theory than practice.
Lende, Helga. *Books about the Blind.* New York: American Foundation for the Blind, 1953.
  References on physical education prior to 1953 are listed.
Los Angeles City Unified School District. *Sequenced Instructional Programs in Physical Education for the Handicapped.* 1970.
  A practical guide for public school physical educators.
Lowenfeld, Berthold. *The Visually Handicapped Child in School.* New York: John Day, 1973.
  Three pages are devoted to physical education. A good reference on other aspects of the education of the blind.
National Education Association. *Teaching Handicapped Students Physical Education.* 1981.
  This is a practical book written for teachers.
Sherrill, Claudine. *Adapted Physical Education and Recreation.* Dubuque, IA: W. C. Brown, 1976.
  Many pages are devoted to blind children with emphasis upon mainstreaming.
Sullivan, Tom. *If You Could See What I Hear.* New York: Harper and Row, 1974.
  The sightless author tells of his experiences in wrestling, water-skiing, sky diving, etc.
United States Association for Blind Athletes. *Athletic Handbook,* edited by David Beaver.
  Policies, rules of competition, and national records are included in the book.
Vannier, Maryhelen. *Physical Activities for the Handicapped.* Englewood Cliffs, NJ: Prentice-Hall, 1976.
  Eight pages are devoted to teaching physical education to blind students.
Vodola, Thomas. *Individualized Physical Education Program for the Handicapped Child.* Englewood Cliffs, NJ: Prentice-Hall, 1973.
  The book is useful for teachers of the multihandicapped.
Wheeler, R. H., and Hooley, A. M. *Physical Education for the Handicapped.* Philadelphia: Lea & Febiger, 1976.
  Seven pages are devoted to the visually impaired.

Whitley, Patricia. *Dr. Charles Buell: Leader in Physical Education for the Visually Impaired, 1980.* Doctoral dissertation, University of North Carolina.

Winnick, J. P., and Short, F. X. *Special Athletic Opportunities for Individuals with Handicapping Conditions.* Brockport, NY: State University College, 1981.

    The book devotes 11 pages to the United States Association for Blind Athletes.

Articles

Buell, Charles. "A Sporting Chance." *Performance.* Feb., 1976.

    Blind athletes in the mainstream is the subject.

Buell, Charles. "Blind Athletes Compete in the Mainstream." *Journal of Visual Impairment and Blindness.* Nov., 1981.

    Gives details and names of athletes.

Buell, Charles. "Blind Wrestlers Win State Championships." *Wrestling USA.* Sept., 1981.

Buell, Charles. "Breaking Through." *Journal of Visual Impairment and Blindness.* Nov., 1981.

    A review of the autobiography of Harry Cordellos.

Buell, Charles. "The First Olympic Games for the Blind." *New Outlook for the Blind.* Dec., 1976.

Buell, Charles. "The First Olympics for the Blind." *Selected Papers 1976, Association for the Education of the Visually Handicapped.* Washington, DC.

    The author describes the experiences of the U.S. team of which he was the manager.

Buell, Charles. "How to Include Blind and Partially Seeing Children in Public Secondary School Vigorous Physical Education." *The Physical Educator.* Mar., 1972.

Buell, Charles. "Mainstreaming Blind Children in Vigorous Physical Education." *Selected Papers of 1978. Association for the Education of the Visually Handicapped.* Washington, DC.

Buell, Charles. *Physical Activities Report.* Old Saybrook, CT: 1977.

    Almost the entire issue is devoted to the integration of blind children into public school physical education. The practical aspects of the program are stressed.

Buell, Charles. "State Championships Won by Blind Wrestlers." *Wrestling USA.* Sept., 1980.

Buell, Charles. "U.S. Swimmers Win Blind Olympics." *Swimming World.* Nov., 1980.

    Refers to international competition in Holland, 1980.

Buell, Charles. "What Wrestling Means to Blind Persons." *Journal of Visual Impairment and Blindness.* Oct., 1977.

    Discusses blind wrestlers in the mainstream of the sport.

Buell, Charles, and Montagnino, A. "Blind Children Integrated into Physical Education Classes in New Jersey Schools." *AAHPERD Update.* Feb., 1976.

    The authors describe the work of a state consultant in physical education for the visually impaired.

Curran, E. A. "Teaching Water Safety Skills to Blind Multihandicapped Children." *Education of the Visually Handicapped.* Mar., 1971.

    A practical program is described in some detail.

DePauw, Karen. "Physical Education for the Visually Impaired: a Review of the Literature." *Journal of Visual Impairment and Blindness.* Apr., 1981.

Dialogue. Winter, 1978. Features recreation for the blind.

Dixon, Judith, "Ski for Light: the Program and the Concept." *Journal of Visual Impairment and Blindness.* Jan., 1979.

Emes, Claudia. "Creative Dance: a Valuable Process for Blind Children." *Education of the Visually Handicapped.* Fall, 1978.

"First Legally Blind Swimmer Competes in National Indoor AAU Meet." *Women's Varsity Sports.* Missoula, MT. Sept., 1981.
> Refers to Trischa Zorn.

Fisher, David. "Blind Students Learn Karate." *Journal of Rehabilitation.* Aug., 1972.

"14 World Marks Broken." *Swimming World.* June, 1979.
> Refers to blind swimmers at National Championships, 1979, of the United States Association for Blind Athletes.

George, C., and Patton, R., "Development of an Aerobic Program for the Visually Impaired." *Journal of Health, Physical Education and Recreation.* May, 1975.

Hartman, R. E. "Ball Games for Visually Impaired Children." *Outlook for the Blind.* Oct., 1974.
> Rules are given for playing some common games.

Holtzworth, Sheila. "The Blind Side of the Mountain." *Mainstream.* Jan., Feb., and Mar., 1982.
> A dairy of climbing Mt. Rainier.

"I Can Do Anything!" *Reader's Digest.* Nov., 1976, pp. 207–14.
> The program offered by Blind Outdoor Leisure Development, Aspen, Colorado is described. Skiing, camping, hiking, fishing, and swimming are mentioned.

Jankowski, L. W., and Evans, J. K., "The Exercise Capacity of Blind Children." *Journal of Visual Impairment and Blindness.* June, 1981.
> This is a study of the physiological characteristics of twenty institutionalized blind children.

Journal of Health, Physical Education and Recreation, Washington, DC: The American Alliance for Health, Physical Education and Recreation. June, 1970.
> Presents a mini-feature on the visually handicapped.

Bolt, M. "The Blind Can Play Softball."

Buell, Charles. "What Is the School's Responsibility in Providing Physical Activity for Its Blind Students?"

Oliver, James. "Physical Education for Blind Children."

Travena, Thomas. "Are Physical Education Programs Meeting the Needs of Students in Public Schools?"

Journal of Health, Physical Education and Recreation. Washington, DC: The American Alliance for Health, Physical Education and Recreation. Apr., 1971.
> Presents a mini-feature on the visually handicapped.

Buell, Charles. "Physical Education for Visually Handicapped Children in Public Schools."

Citron, Lester. "Tin Cans and Blind Kids."

Johansen, Gladys. "Integrating Visually Handicapped Children into Public Elementary School Physical Education Programs."

Miller, Oral. "Blind Bowling."

Kearney, S., and Copeland, R. "Goal Ball." *Journal of Health, Physical Education and Recreation.* Sept., 1979.
> Gives the rules of goal ball.

Kimbrough, Louise. "U.S. Wins Blind Olympics." *Dialogue.* Fall, 1980.

Krebs, Kathryn. "Hatha Yoga for Visually Impaired Students." *Journal of Visual Impairment and Blindness.* June, 1979.

Laughlin, Sheila. "A Walking-Jogging Program for Blind Persons." *New Outlook for the Blind.* Sept., 1975.
> A program using a 220-yard oval track with a rail is described.

Loeschke, M. "Mime: a Movement Program for the Visually Handicapped." *Journal of Visual Impairment and Blindness.* Oct., 1977.

Describes an experimental study to determine whether mime techniques are useful for teaching movement to visually impaired students.

"Masters of Wrestling Award." *Wrestling USA.* June, 1980.
  Tells of the contributions to wrestling of Charles Buell.

McKay, Nathan. "Notes on Jogging." *New Outlook for the Blind.* Sept., 1973.

National Junior Geographic. Feb., 1979.
  Has a story for children on athletics for the blind.

Nezol, James. "Physical Education for Integrated Blind Students: Its Relationship to Socio-Metric Status and Recreational Activity Choices." *Education of the Visually Handicapped.* Mar., 1972.
  Blind children who participate in vigorous physical education in public schools gain the respect of their sighted peers.

Osmun, Mark. "Inner Vision." *The Runner.* Nov., 1978.
  Tells the story of blind marathoner, Harry Cordellos.

Parker, Elizabeth. "Movement Exploration and Gymnastics for Visually Handicapped Children." *Selected Papers for 1972, Association for the Education of the Visually Handicapped.*

Pitzer, J. "Nordic Ski Touring for the Visually Handicapped." *Education of the Visually Handicapped.* May, 1974.

Pitzer, J., and Sonka, J. "Leisure Time Activities for the Visually Impaired." *Journal of Health, Physical Education and Recreation.* Oct., 1974.

Pomeroy, Janet. "Recreation for Severely Handicapped Persons in a Community Center." *New Outlook for the Blind.* Feb., 1972.

"The Quietest Game in Town." *Dialogue.* Spring, 1978.
  The game is beep baseball.

Rachun, Alexius. "Vision and Sports." *Sight Saving Review 38:4.*
  Only a few eye conditions can be aggravated by vigorous physical activity.

Rand, Marcia. "Dance and Creative Movement for Blind Persons." *New Outlook for the Blind.* Feb., 1973.

Resnick, Rose. "Creative Movement Classes for Visually Handicapped Children in a Public School Setting." *New Outlook for the Blind.* Dec., 1973.
  Emphasis is placed on motor skills, posture, and orientation.

Resnick, Rose. "Recreation: a Gateway to the Seeing World." *New Outlook for the Blind.* Nov., 1971.

Spittler, Margaret. "Games for the Development of Pre-orientation and Mobility Skills." *New Outlook for the Blind.* Dec., 1975.
  Twelve games which can be played by blind and sighted children are described.

Stamford, B. "A Cardiovascular Endurance Training for Blind Persons." *New Outlook for the Blind.* Sept., 1975.
  Stair-stepping exercises are discussed.

Stephens, Roberta. "Running Free: the Use of a 'Running Cable' with Blind Adolescents Who Function on a Retarded Level." *New Outlook for the Blind.* Dec., 1973.
  Use of a running cable in a hospital setting is discussed.

"Swimmer Overcomes Visual Impairment." *Women's Varsity Sports.* Missoula, MT, Nov., 1979.

Turner, R., and Biblars, A. "Blind People Can Do More than Tread Water." *Braille Monitor.* Berkeley, CA: National Federation of the Blind, Nov. 1971.
  Scuba diving is discussed.

Vletze, Dorothy. "Profile in Courage." *International Gymnast.* Dec., 1978.
  Tells of blind gymnast on high school team.

Wilson, John. "The Blind Climbers of Kilimanjaro." *The Seer.* Harrisburg, PA: Pennsylvania Association for the Blind, Sept., 1970.

Magazines and Newsletters

Feeling Sports. 7525 North St., Minneapolis, MN 55426. A 4-page newsletter.

Teen-Time. Concord Publishing House, 3558 S. Jefferson Ave., St. Louis, MO 63118.
    Braille and large type editions are available at no cost. Monthly sports column on sports for the blind.

USABA Newsletter. United States Association for Blind Athletes, 55 W. California Ave., Beach Haven Park, NJ 08008.
    Available to members who pay $7.00 annual dues. News of regional, national, and international sports for the blind. Some mainstreaming items are also included.

Films

The Bold Challenge. Blind Outdoor Leisure Development, Aspen, CO. A film on teaching skiing.

Focus on Ability. American Red Cross. The subject is teaching swimming to the handicapped, including blind individuals.

Mainstreaming in Physical Education for the Blind. Campbell Films, Saxtons River, VT 05154. An 18-minute film "shot" in public schools, 1978.

A Matter of Inconvenience. Stanfield House, 900 Euclid Ave., Santa Monica, CA 90403. Blind and amputee skiers are shown.

Not without Sight. American Foundation for the Blind, 15 W. 16th St., New York, NY 10011. Using novel effects the film shows what individuals with various eye conditions see.

Out of Left Field. American Foundation for the Blind, 15 W. 16th St., New York, NY 10011. The film is devoted to integrating blind children into community recreation.

Physical Education and Recreation for the Blind. College of Health, Physical Education and Recreation, Texas Woman's University, Denton, TX 76201. A casette tape comes with 80 slides.

Physical Education for Blind Children. Campbell Films, Saxtons River, VT 05154. A 20-minute film covering many activities of school children of all ages.

Survival Run. Magus Films, 117 S. Park St., San Francisco, CA 94107. Available only by purchase. The film is 12 minutes long showing Harry Cordellos, totally blind, and a sighted partner running the most difficult cross-country trail in America. It is very inspirational and has won many film awards.

Education and Problems of Blind Persons

American Foundation for the Blind Directory of Agencies. New York: The Foundation, 1981.

American Printing House for the Blind. *Annual Report,* 1981. Louisville, KY.

Bishop, Virginia. *Teaching the Visually Limited Child.* Springfield, IL: Charles C. Thomas, 1971.

Carroll, T. *Blindness: What It Is, What It Does, and How to Live with It.* Boston: Little, Brown, 1961.

Chevigny, H., *My Eyes Have a Cold Nose.* New Haven, CT: Yale Press, 1946.

Cohn, O. "Prejudice and the Blind." In L.F. Lukoff's *Attitudes toward Blind Persons.* New York: American Foundation for the Blind, 1972.

Cutsforth, Thomas. *The Blind in School and Society.* New York: American Foundation for the Blind, 1957.

Dickman, Irving. *Living with Blindness*. Public Affairs Pamphlets, 381 Park Ave. S., New York, NY 10016.

Halliday, C., and Kurzhals, I.W. *Stimulating Environments for Children Who Are Visually Impaired*. Springfield, IL: Charles C. Thomas, 1976.

Hill, E., and Ponder, P. *Orientation and Mobility Techniques: a Guide for the Practitioner*. New York: American Foundation for the Blind, 1976.

Irwin, Robert. *As I Saw It*. New York: American Foundation for the Blind, 1955.

Josephson, E. *The Social Life of Blind People*. New York: American Foundation for the Blind, 1968.

Kastein, S.; Spaulding, L.; and Scharf, B. *Raising the Young Blind Child: a Guide for Parents and Educators*. New York: Human Science Press, 1980.

Lowenfeld, B. *Our Blind Children*. 3d ed. Springfield, IL: Charles C. Thomas, 1971.

Lukoff, I. F., and Cohn, O. *Attitudes toward Blind Persons*. New York: American Foundation for the Blind, 1972.

Monbeck, M. *The Meaning of Blindness: Attitudes toward Blindness and Blind People*. Bloomington, IN: Indiana University Press, 1973.

Rusalem, H. *Coping with the Unseen Environment*. New York: Columbia Teachers College Press, 1972.

Schlitz, C., ed. *A Curriculum Guide for the Development of Body and Sensory Awareness for the Visually Impaired*. Illinois Office of Education, 1974.

Scott, R. *The Making of Blind Men*. New York: Russell Sage, 1969.

Seligman, M. *Strategies for Helping Parents of Exceptional Children*. New York: The Free Press.

Twersky, J. *The Sound of the Walls*. Garden City, NY: Doubleday & Co., 1959.

Webster, P. *The Road to Freedom: a Parent's Guide to Travel Independently*. Illinois: Katan, 1977.

Welsh, R., and Blasch, B. *Foundations of Orientation and Mobility*. New York: American Foundation for the Blind, 1980.

Yeadon, R., and Grayson, D. *Living with Impaired Vision: an Introduction*. American Foundation for the Blind, 1979.

Zahl, P., ed., *Blindness*. Princeton, NJ: Princeton University Press, 1950.

About the Author

In 1974 Dr. Charles Buell retired from 40 years of teaching the visually impaired in residential schools for the blind and in public schools. Although he is himself legally blind, he was a pioneer in physical education and recreation for the visually handicapped, has written extensively about all aspects of these programs, and has developed films on physical education for the blind. For 28 years he has edited a newsletter for the Association for the Education of the Visually Handicapped. He lectures and leads demonstrations of activities and methods for universities and school districts all over the country. He received the AAHPER Anderson Award for these and other contributions in 1974.

Dr. Buell was the Manager of the first U.S. Olympic team of blind athletes. He was instrumental in organizing the United States Association for Blind Athletes in 1976, and is Editor of the *USABA Newsletter*.